To Shelly –
with best wishes
Newt
4/24/71

MAKING
THE BEST OF IT

MAKING THE BEST OF IT

A COMMON-SENSE GUIDE TO NEGOTIATING A DIVORCE

Newton Frohlich

HARPER & ROW, PUBLISHERS

1817

New York, Evanston, San Francisco, London

TO MARTHA

 For information address Harper & Row, Publishers, Inc., 49 East 33rd Street, New York, N.Y. 10016. Published simultaneously in Canada by Fitzhenry & Whiteside Limited, Toronto.

FIRST EDITION

STANDARD BOOK NUMBER: 06-011373-1

LIBRARY OF CONGRESS CATALOG CARD NUMBER: 72-138724

CONTENTS

ACKNOWLEDGMENTS

There are many people whom I must thank for their assistance and encouragement. My friend, Joseph Borkin, Washington attorney and author, was from the day I started to write this book an enthusiastic debater, gadfly and critic. If, according to Herbert Marcuse, Joe was the primal father of *Eros and Civilization*, then Joe was certainly the primal uncle of this book.

I owe my friend, Andrew J. Glass, congressional correspondent for the *National Journal*, the special thanks of someone who has just experienced the joys of learning a new skill from a real pro. And from his wife, Dr. Eleanor A. Sorrentino, a Washington, D.C., psychiatrist, I have gained much insight into the problems of troubled people in divorce.

ACKNOWLEDGMENTS

To my partners, especially my senior partner, Sidney S. Sachs, and Leonard C. Greenebaum, with whom I have practiced so congenially over the years, I am grateful for the opportunity of sharing with them the many problems encountered by us in the practice of law.

Many other people have been kind enough to read this manuscript and give me their suggestions. Among them are Mr. Arnold Barach, Senior Editor, Kiplinger's "Changing Times"; Hon. Harry Batshaw, Associate Justice, Superior Court of Montreal; Mr. James Fitzpatrick, member of the law firm of Arnold & Porter; Dr. Alec C. Levin; Mr. Roderick MacLeish, Foreign Correspondent, Westinghouse Broadcasting Corporation; Mr. Laurence Stern, Assistant Managing Editor, The Washington *Post;* and Mr. Lester Tanzer, General Editor, *U.S. News & World Report.* Erwin Mendelson, C.P.A., carefully checked the tax computations for which I thank him.

And to my parents, May and William Frohlich, I owe a special acknowledgment. They taught me the ambience of "family" and a special appreciation for what a happy marriage is all about; my mother typed the manuscript, and my father, an attorney of many years' experience, gave me the benefit of his insight and research.

To Ann Harris and Jay Iselin, my editors at Harper & Row, I state my sincere appreciation for their enthusiastic guidance.

To my dear wife, Martha, I give special thanks for her helpful criticism and her cheerful cooperation while I worked on this book.

To my children, Nina and Jimmy, I offer my hope that they will join Martha and me in never becoming one of those for whom reading *Making the Best of It* has too personal a relevance.

N. F.

PREFACE

The purpose of this book is to show that there is a way to divorce that is private, reasonable and straightforward—and almost completely within the control of the husband and wife.

Divorce today resembles more a negotiated agreement than the sordid kind of melodramatic courtroom trial shown on television. Therefore, any spouse about to start the process of divorcing should be armed with the skills of bargaining, the knowledge of how to use psychological counseling in the negotiating process, the benefits that the tax laws provide for divorced people, the pitfalls that private detectives can bring to the divorce bargainer and the wisdom to appreciate the delicate position the children hold in the negotiating process.

PREFACE

The crux of this book is that the process of getting a divorce, if handled rightly, will not add "insult to injury." I neither try to expose (nor play on) the pain of those involved, nor do I propose that the process of dissolving a marriage is a do-it-yourself enterprise. Instead, my purpose is to try to remove the fear of the process itself from those who have already decided that their marriage is dead.

For years, I have seen hundreds of people pass through my law office in Washington in search of a solution to their unhappy marriage. For such people, the most desirable solution would be to save their marriage and see it grow into a happy one. Unfortunately, I have found no formula to reach that goal. Nor is it my purpose to encourage them to divorce. My goal is simply to write a book for those million persons who each year conclude that they must divorce and to tell them that there is a fairer and more decent way to go about getting a divorce than the notorious ones they have heard about.

January, 1971
Chevy Chase, Maryland

NEWTON FROHLICH

[1]

MAKING THE BEST OF IT

Day after day, unhappy men and women enter lawyers' offices expecting the worst. They want a divorce. Their marriage is no longer happy, and they are sure a sordid ordeal lies ahead of them. They fear that their divorce must be fought out in a bitter courtroom trial in which their bedroom behavior and personal finances will become public knowledge.

But they are wrong.

They believe they must have "grounds" for divorce—that they must actually "prove" that their husband or wife has been cruel to them or deserted them. They think of a divorce as an expensive war in which conniving lawyers and dictatorial judges make the rules.

Again, they are wrong.

If you are thinking of getting a divorce, or are in the process of obtaining one, you can save yourself a lot of grief and probably a lot of money too if you come to look upon what is happening as a private arrangement. When you do, the chances are that your divorce can be negotiated in your living room or in the privacy of your lawyer's office and the only time you will have to appear in court is when the divorce decree is actually granted.

The other alternatives are apt to be grim: the phony courtroom show often portrayed on daytime television, or the real-life drama in which a husband or wife sets in motion a chain of uncertain, unhappy and wasteful moves, none of which can possibly benefit either of them—large attorneys' fees, children who are hurt and resent their parents for dragging them through court, and the rest of the heavy legal baggage that weighs down a contested divorce.

As best you can, try to look on divorce—yours or anybody else's—as a dissolution of an unsuccessful partnership, a sad job to be done, but a task more productive than wasteful. Today, divorce can be a time for private reassessment and planning rather than a period of public spectacle and a seemingly endless torture. Today, divorce can be accomplished with less fear and fanfare.

A couple I shall call (with no particular originality) Mr. and Mrs. Jones found this out. I'm telling their story (parts of which may be similar to your experiences) in the hope that you can profit from their mistakes and from their eventual success in negotiating instead of fighting.

When Mrs. Jones called her lawyer, she had discovered that her husband had been sleeping with a woman every time he visited Pittsburgh for a monthly sales trip. She triumphantly threw on his desk six incriminating motel receipts she had found.

MAKING THE BEST OF IT

It seemed so simple—an open-and-shut case of adultery, clear grounds for divorce.

But was it so simple? When her lawyer asked her whether she had had sexual relations with her husband since she learned of his adultery, she said "yes." He told her that having relations with her husband after she learned of his unfaithfulness could be interpreted in a courtroom as forgiveness and that, therefore, she would have no grounds for divorce.

Meanwhile, her husband had heard that his wife had consulted a lawyer. (He had been waiting for this ever since he found his "Mr. and Mrs." motel receipts in disarray.) Now it was Mr. Jones's turn to see a lawyer in "self-defense." If she wants a divorce, he announced, it's all right with me. But, he warned, he would never pay her any alimony. The only ones he would support were his two young children. And, what's more, he would not pay any high legal fees. Now the battle began in earnest:

Mrs. Jones wanted to draw all the money out of their joint bank accounts.

Mr. Jones wanted to close all the charge accounts.

Mrs. Jones wanted to keep Mr. Jones from ever visiting the children after the divorce.

Mr. Jones claimed his wife was frigid and wanted to know if the judge would give any weight to this contention.

Mrs. Jones wondered if she should hire a detective.

Mr. Jones threatened to leave town and send her only what money he wanted to.

At this point, Mr. and Mrs. Jones appear to be headed for an old-fashioned tragic divorce-court divorce, but the courthouse battle never occurred. All because they got some sound advice —and took it. They negotiated their divorce.

Mr. Jones swore at first that he would never pay alimony to

Mrs. Jones. But, ultimately, he *wanted* to pay some alimony because of the clear tax benefits to him that such payments hold.

Mrs. Jones was ready to fight to the end to prevent her husband from ever seeing the children. But she struck a much more productive bargain: she agreed to having her former husband take the children for a long summer vacation trip each year with his new wife—in return for his agreement to pay for their college education.

How long did Mr. and Mrs. Jones take to negotiate their divorce? Eight and one-half months.

How long did the actual divorce trial take? Five or ten minutes.

What were the grounds for divorce? Whatever required the least emotionally charged testimony. (In the case of the Joneses, they used "voluntary separation," the ground that is most commonly used in such negotiated divorce cases in the area where they lived.)

What Is "Negotiated Divorce"?

"Negotiated divorce" is the process by which a husband and wife—with the help of their lawyers—quietly and privately discuss the problems of dissolving their marriage: Should they separate? Should they divorce? Can they reconcile? Can psychological or psychiatric counseling help? Who shall have custody of the children? On what days should be the visitations of the husband with the children? How much child support should he pay? Should he also pay alimony to the wife? Who gets the house and the furniture? Should any of it be sold? What insurance should be continued? Who will pay for the college education of the children?

The divorcing husbands and wives answer these questions through a process of bargaining and compromise. Their lawyers guide them by advancing each side's best arguments, by using such leverage as each can muster and, finally, by reducing their agreements to writing in a document called a Separation Agreement. This agreement authorizes the husband and wife to separate and live apart from each other and sets out in black and white their comprehensive plan for the future management of one family under two roofs. It covers such matters as the bank accounts, the children, support and alimony, college education, life insurance, medical bills and summer vacations.

The "Non-trial" of a Negotiated Divorce

Once the separation agreement is signed, they go about getting their divorce. Across the United States, most people use some form of "cruelty" or "desertion" or "incompatibility" or "living apart" or "intolerable treatment" as the "ground" for divorce. But these are only words. It really doesn't matter what term they use. In most cases, only one of the family, the husband or the wife, need appear in court although both lawyers are there to make certain all interests are protected. The testimony is spiceless and unchallenged, the "trial" a mere formality. What is important is that the judge has a chance to be sure the separation agreement is fair and reasonable.

Their case is usually one of perhaps twenty that have been scheduled for the judge to hear that day. All have been labeled "uncontested" by the parties involved.

For reasons of chivalry more than anything else, the wife—more often than the husband—is the one who "gets" the divorce. She is called to the witness stand to testify. In response to her lawyer's questions, she gives her name, address and how long she has been living in the state and county. Then, gently led by her attorney, she blandly describes, if her grounds for divorce are to be "cruelty," how her husband has been cruel to her. Often her description of cruelty is limited to the simple conclusion that her husband was "cool and indifferent" to her. Sometimes state law requires that she have suffered physically at his hands. So she describes the sleep (or, if she is lucky, the weight) she has lost. Sometimes she may describe the number of tranquilizers she had to take as a result of her husband's aggravating conduct. Generally, however, the wife can obtain the divorce with a simple rendition of the "cool and indifferent" formulistic recital.

After she has completed her testimony, her lawyer hands her the signed separation and property settlement agreement.

He asks her if the signatures on the last page are actually those of herself and her husband.

He asks her if she has read and understands the contents of the agreement.

He asks her if she had a lawyer throughout the period she was negotiating the agreement.

He asks her if she signed it freely and voluntarily—without anyone forcing her.

He asks her if she is satisfied with the provisions of the agreement.

He asks her if she thinks the agreement is reasonable.

Of course, the wife answers "yes" to each of the questions. The judge need not sit on the edge of his seat to follow the dialogue. But he is on guard for a hesitation on the part of the wife—or, in a rare case, a resounding "no" to any of those questions. For a judge's key function in today's divorce trial is to be certain that no one has been forced into signing a separation agreement, and that each side understands what has happened.

So, the judge today stands as society's watchdog—guarding against the intrusion of coercion and fraud into the private negotiations of a husband and wife. If you try to "put one over" on your spouse or to intimidate your spouse into not obtaining a separate lawyer, in most cases, a judge will detect unfairness in the proceedings and refuse to allow the divorce.

One last formality still remains: a friend or relative must also take the witness stand to assure the judge that the wife is indeed a resident of the state and was actually treated cruelly by the husband. She must also assure the judge that the wife is fit to have custody of the children. The friend then steps down from the witness chair. The divorce trial is over.

The judge then decrees the divorce. To a divorcing husband and wife the trial has been somewhat like a delayed funeral for a marriage long since dead. For them, the marriage died when *they* decided to end it and not when the judge granted the decree. They went about the job of dissolving all the ties that bound them—in their own way, without the help of the judge.

As a result, only a small minority of the million Americans who divorce each year need go to Reno or Las Vegas. Mexican "quickie" divorces are less and less common. Approximately eight out of every ten of the husbands and wives who obtain divorces today do so in their own home state. Today, in every state, the time it takes to get a divorce depends for the most part on how long it takes a husband and wife to negotiate their separation agreement. Only the statutory waiting period in some states between separating (or filing the separation agreement, or obtaining a judicial separation decree) and getting the actual decree of divorce interferes with a couple having total control over the time they take to obtain a divorce.

Today, the real passport to divorce is *not* the divorce decree. It is the *separation agreement.* And in the end, when the divorce decree is finally obtained, a divorced family has more for its anguish, money and effort than memories of a divorce court and a justice they thought they did not receive.

Why Is Negotiated Divorce So Popular?

When you come to think about it, the widespread and increasing popularity of negotiated divorce is easy to understand. Once the emotional block is hurdled, it becomes attractive because it allows unhappy couples to handle by *themselves*—with the help of their lawyers—the task of reorganizing their lives and budgets instead of delegating this job to an overworked judge. It is attractive because it encourages people to control their emotional problems long enough to disentangle themselves from an unhappy marriage and to avoid the destructive and unproductive game of fixing blame before a courtroom of strangers.

With the current high rate of divorce, any other system would impose an impossibly staggering burden on our courts.

Imagine what chaos would result if the 500,000 couples who want a divorce each year had to wait their turn to appear before a judge and each case was fought out in a long, contested courtroom proceeding.

Fortunately, today's "courtroom divorces" are strictly in the minority. They occur when a husband has reason to challenge the wife's ability to raise the children properly because of her mental illness—or her sexual promiscuity—or when the wife fears the husband will expose the children to his "world of girl friends." These contested divorce cases are also found when the husband and wife use a fight over custody or visits—or money—as a way of getting back at each other. They use the children—or money—as pawns in a sick game which they themselves start, only to blame the messy trial (or the unsatisfactory decision that results) on the inept lawyer, the biased judge or the mysterious "divorce racket."

This does not mean that fighting in court about such matters as alimony or visitation rights is always avoidable or always undesirable. It does, after all, take two to negotiate. Moreover, litigation—threatened or actual—can be an effective lever in the process of negotiating a divorce—particularly when a husband or wife refuses to come to the bargaining table.

Yet, even in these cases—in which there appears to be some justification for taking the divorce to court or when litigation is simply unavoidable—the results are rarely worth it. Men have been known to pontificate—after the battle—about how the divorce system is merely an instrument of women to punish men. Women have been known to whine—after an ineffective attempt to get more alimony than they need (or their husband can afford)—about how the divorce system is a tool of the men and their male judges to take advantage of the weaker sex.

Men have blamed the loss of a meaningful relationship with their children on the divorce system rather than on themselves. Women have blamed their worsened financial condition on a miserly ex-husband or on a lawyer who did not know how to bring him to his knees, rather than on facing, realistically, the circumstances of their life.

But these are people who handle the problems of their divorce with the same thoughtlessness with which they handled the problems of marriage and with the same result—failure.

Negotiated Divorce Is Not a Self-Help Device

Negotiated divorce is not a self-help device that husbands and wives can manage by themselves. In light of the underlying problems that have led to the need for a divorce, it makes good sense to get outside help.

Even the best-intentioned husbands and wives, determined to negotiate their divorce without help from lawyers, encounter major problems.

For example, let's assume you are a husband who wants to be as financially generous with your wife and children as you can possibly be. Still, your idea of what is "generous" may not be the same as your wife's and, in any event, someone must ultimately decide what you can afford to pay. Will you make the ultimate decision? Or will your wife?

Even if you can agree on how much alimony and support is to be paid, who will decide how much of the total sum will be allocated between alimony and child support? Allocation is important. Alimony payments can be deducted by husbands on their tax returns; child support payments cannot. Of course, you would like to get as fat a tax deduction as possible. On the other hand, your wife will have to pay the tax bill on all the alimony she receives. Besides, alimony ends when she remarries—and eight out of ten women remarry. She will be asking for trouble if she receives too much alimony; it might be better for her to receive more child support.

Or, let's assume you are a wife who wants her husband to see the children as much as possible after the divorce. Yet, you don't want him dropping in whenever he feels like it. After all, separation from your ex-husband is the least of the benefits you're expecting from divorce. Who decides how many visits are enough, and with what spacing, and on what notice? You, or he?

The point is that there are many subtle and complex factors that must be decided and the best—and sometimes only—way to do that is through compromise. Since compromising comes hardest when both sides force themselves to do it face to face, you need a lawyer.

Some divorcing couples have a trusted friend or friends to whom they can presumably turn for support and advice. But these friends run the risk of being accused of "taking sides," failing as counselors and ultimately losing the husband, the wife, or both as friends.

Even if the friends were to surmount all these dangers, it is not a wise policy to arrange the terms of your divorce through them because, ninety-nine times out of a hundred, your friends simply will not have sufficient knowledge and experience in dealing with varieties of methods of settling all the many problems inherent in a divorce. A good lawyer, of course, has this knowledge at his fingertips and, what's more, he is far less likely to become emotionally involved in the problem and thus is more apt to offer sounder and more objective advice than an "old friend."

Do Not Look for Just a "Divorce Lawyer"

Selecting the right lawyer is crucial. He has to be the kind of person you can talk to in a forthright and honest way. Moreover, his approach to handling divorce cases can make a great difference. Since divorces generally are negotiated, your lawyer should be adept at the art of negotiation. (He should *also* know how to handle himself in the courtroom and he should have a command of all procedural intricacies of litigation, in case, despite your best joint efforts, the divorce proceedings go to court.)

There is no sure way to find the "right" lawyer. The most helpful advice is to examine the lawyer's reputation. Inquire among your friends, business associates, religious counselors, doctor or "marriage counselor" for the names of lawyers who, to their best knowledge, have skillfully and prudently handled divorce actions.

Do not ask for just a "divorce lawyer." Someone might refer you to a lawyer who has a reputation for performing in the courtroom but may know next to nothing about tax law or the other subtle points inherent in a good negotiation effort.

Neither should you ask for just a good negotiator. You might just be setting yourself up for a passive armchair bargainer who will bargain away all your rights. (Since the other side knows he's not the type who's likely to go to court, it might take full advantage of this weakness in pressing its case.)

So you should seek a lawyer who is a *good negotiator* as well as a *good litigator*, who is known for his *reasonableness*, as well as his *firmness*, and who has an awareness of tax problems as well as marital problems. This, admittedly, is not an easy task but such lawyers *do* exist and, with diligence, they can be found and retained.

Do not be afraid to "shop around" a bit if you feel uncertain. If you are referred to a lawyer whose approach and personality strike you amiss in your preliminary meeting, do not hesitate to look elsewhere. This may cost you some extra "consultation fees" but the experience—and the resulting relationship with a lawyer who fully meets your needs—is well worth the extra time and money. You are dealing with *your* future and the future of your family.

From the Very Beginning, Consider Negotiating—Not Litigating

Today, nine out of every ten couples who get a divorce in America end up by negotiating the terms of their separation and their divorce. Sometimes, they try to negotiate by themselves first. Sometimes, they start by litigating. But, sooner or later they negotiate through their lawyers and make a careful deal in dissolving their marriage. If the percentages indicate that sooner or later you too will want to negotiate your divorce, why not start off in the right way from the very beginning?

Your problems will not end when you select a good lawyer. He can litigate and negotiate for you but, in the end, you are the one who must make the decisions. Have you and your spouse consulted long enough with the psychiatric or psychological counselors? Have you received the full benefit of their help in trying to save your marriage or, if that is no longer possible, to ease your way toward divorce? Have you been holding out in the negotiations for a relatively unimportant item, wasting your energies and money, and forgetting to bargain for an important tax provision or child visitation control? Do you really need to hire a private detective? Do you really need "grounds" for divorce? Must you really worry about taking the time and spending the money to go to Reno in order to obtain your divorce quickly, unceremoniously and privately?

These questions—and many more—cannot be answered glibly. Nor are the questions—much less the answers—always the same for husbands and for wives. But if you realize the facts of life—that today's divorces are generally negotiated—and you prepare for divorce with this knowledge clearly in mind, the answers to your particular problems will come more easily, and the process will become less frightening.

[2]

THE DIVORCE COUNSELORS

> It is hard for a free fish to understand what is happening to a hooked one.
>
> —KARL A. MENNINGER

Logically, the first place to start a discussion of the process of negotiated divorce is with the marriage itself. How did the trouble start? What went wrong? Is divorce the answer?

Most people who are unhappy in marriage need to talk about it. Some talk to friends. But, increasingly, more and more people are seeking psychological guidance and understanding with the hope that they can save their marriage. Today, more often than not, unhappy spouses look for psychological help before they look for a lawyer. If not, the lawyer they choose is likely to suggest counseling as the first step they should take. This is because it is recognized as being crucial to the success of negotiated divorce.

The people unhappy spouses consult can generally be called

marriage counselors though, as we will see, they may have various titles. Possibly they will be able to save some marriages. But even when they cannot, they still have value. Often they can help you accept the painful awareness that your marriage is beyond help. They may be able to aid you in learning why your marriage failed and what you can do to avoid repeating the same mistakes. They can change your focus from despair and failure to the possibility of re-creating a new life for yourself. They can disarm emotional bombs quietly, in the privacy of their offices, rather than allow them to explode in the courtroom. Marriage counselors can help—even if they end up counseling divorce rather than marriage. There is nothing disparaging, then, in also calling them "divorce counselors."

This chapter provides a glimpse into who they are, how much they charge, what methods they use and how they fit into the process of negotiated divorce.

Who Are the Divorce Counselors?

Divorce counselors have many names. Some are psychiatrists—medical doctors who specialize in problems of mental health. Others are medical doctors who are not specialists in this area, but who are still awfully good at counseling married couples. Some are psychologists who do not have a medical degree, but have undergone specialized training in the psychological problems of personal relationships. Some are social workers; others are psychotherapists; some are pastoral counselors; others are actually called marriage counselors. Some psychologists are marriage counselors but not all marriage counselors are psychologists. Some counselors call themselves therapists, others call themselves analysts. While some are skilled professionals, others are counselors in name only, clerks in the courthouses who interview spouses who have filed suits for divorce and go through the verbal paces of attempting to reconcile couples with varying degrees of success. In other words, anyone can put up a shingle and call himself a "marriage counselor."

Many people never get to a marriage counselor as such, but go to a clergyman or lawyer when their marriage founders and still have been "counseled" by an expert in marriage counseling.

Finding a Good Psychological Counselor: Criteria, Cost and Techniques

Just as there is no one definition of what is a "divorce counselor," there is no one criterion for finding a good "divorce counselor." Generally speaking, the best assistance comes from psychiatrists and psychologists. Your lawyer usually can give you several names. So can the psychiatric department of a local medical school, or a religious or a social service agency.

"Divorce counselors" try to overcome your disabling feelings of guilt and fear. They try to develop in you a sense of confidence and self-respect through which these emotions can be conquered. They try to break the pattern of loneliness. They try to make it clearer to you why your marriage has failed. When you understand why, you will be able to cope with your marriage more realistically even if it should mean negotiating an end to it. The guilt and fear that choke you have a chance to change into understanding. Your emotions, which used to breed only the urge to run away or to squabble, can gradually begin to breed different urges: to love again, to be ambitious, to be confident.

The cost of this kind of help can range from $15 at a religious or governmental social service agency to as much as $50 an hour charged by some psychologists and psychiatrists.

The psychiatric and psychological counselors utilize many approaches. Some will see the husband and wife together and then supplement those visits with separate sessions. Other psychologists and psychiatrists prefer to see only one spouse—alone. Still others see both spouses but in separate visits over the same period of time. Others will see both spouses not only at separate times but during separate periods, that is, the wife separately for a few months, then the husband separately for a few months. Some believe in what they call collaborative therapy: two therapists seeing one partner. Others believe in two therapists meeting simultaneously with the two spouses. Still others follow a program of group therapy. (This is an increasingly popular program—both with therapists and spouses.)

Often the couple starts with preliminary interviews with a psychologist, for example, and then joins a group of from five to as many as fifteen spouses with one or two therapists. They work out their problems jointly. Such group sessions are less expensive than private sessions and can be just as successful.

Each counselor has his own means of communication during therapy sessions.* For the most part, what goes on in these sessions is talk: painful, helpful, sometimes even happy. Sometimes, of course, they are just a waste of time—particularly when the husband or wife refuses to make even the smallest invest-

*Not long ago an article in *Life* magazine reported on "Model Railroad Therapy." A New York psychiatrist built an electric train set in his office with two sets of controls. The husband and wife were each asked to operate one of the sets. The object was to see what choices the husband and wife made—long roundabout routes that take time or short direct ones that run the risk of collision. The therapist was also interested in learning whether they worked out their mutual problems of getting their respective trains to the end of the line before their time was up by retreat, compromise or full-throttle bluff.

ment in the success of the session. An uncommunicative spouse, who refuses to work at it at all, enters counseling for the sole purpose of being able to tell the rest of the world that "I've done everything to save my marriage, even to the point of going to a marriage counselor." Counseling can be productive, of course, only if both parties are cooperative with the counselor's professional efforts to broaden understanding.

Is Your Counselor Divorce or Marriage Oriented?

Some counselors are clearly "marriage oriented" and their avowed goal is to keep the marriage together. Other counselors are clearly "person oriented" with the avowed goal of helping the individual patient to overcome his or her emotional disruption or "hangup" even if it means the eventual destruction of the marriage. Between these divergent attitudes are many counselors whose orientation is not so clearly defined.

You may not know whether you are seeing a counselor whose goal is to keep the marriage intact or a counselor whose goal is to keep you in one piece, regardless of what happens to your marriage.

If you have sought counseling in an effort to keep your foundering marriage together, you may be frustrated to learn that you are suffering from neurotic behavior and should try to change that behavior. In the process of change, your otherwise subsisting marriage may be ruined. Such spouses, before trying to rid themselves of neuroses, should examine whether or not their neuroses "dovetail" with the neuroses of their mate.* Some-

*For many spouses, the best thing may be a marriage in which one spouse's "hangups" mesh with the other's. As one Washington, D.C. psychiatrist once put it, "The rocks in his head match the holes in hers." Many a husband and wife can continue to live together acceptably for years along parallel but noncommunicating lines, with little interchange of feelings, spending little time together, even though they share the same house, and perhaps the same bed.

times, too, the counselors find that the marriage has become a problem because personalities change during the course of marriage. Dr. Marc H. Hollander observes:

> It is sometimes stated that one partner in a marriage *matures*, while the other does not. For example, a woman with many fears of men, especially in regard to sex, might choose a very non-assertive, even meek man. After a few years she may become less fearful, and then long for a more assertive, even a more romantic man. Divorce and remarriage may be the outcome. It would seem to me to be more accurate to state that she has *changed* rather than matured.

Often, personalities which have showed little change before therapy change during therapy. Many a man who is insecure and who is unhappy in his marriage has not been able to find the courage to break out of the marriage. He knows the marriage is bad for him. He knows that even if he has problems, his wife has problems too and they clash. He goes to a psychiatrist. He may tell himself and his wife he is going to help make their marriage a better one. But in the process he gains confidence, insight into his problems, and the courage to do something about them. Often the problems are insoluble—and that "something" is divorce.

Divorce Counseling and the Children

In these sessions, husbands and wives, while learning about themselves and their marriage, often come to realize that their children may be better off with a divorce. Ideally, of course, children are best off in a happy home in which both parents live and love. But unhappy spouses have come to recognize, largely through counseling, that a serene broken home may be better for their children than an unhappy unbroken home. In a divorced home with parental love, there is a chance for tranquility and security. Parents who stay together under loveless and discordant circumstances are likely to see their children grow in size but be damaged in psyche.

All this does not mean that divorce is the foolproof way to make your children happier. For one thing, divorce does not necessarily end parental bickering. "Children who face the loss of a parent through divorce must deal with not only the separation," according to Drs. Norman Bernstein and James S. Robey of the Department of Psychiatry and Pediatrics, at Harvard Medical School, "but also with the continuing anger between their fathers and mothers."

Moreover, almost anyone who has been divorced knows how difficult it can be for young boys to develop masculine traits in a fatherless house. Most of them learn, of course, but more slowly than in families where there is a father present. Sometimes, too, a resentful mother consciously or unconsciously distorts the picture of the absent father. She may tell her children about how badly she has been treated by their father, unaware that when she does so she is emotionally damaging her son.

Drs. Bernstein and Robey have reported that children from broken homes often feel responsible for the trouble, and will say this readily to outsiders. Also, "fears and dreams that are universal among children take on new meanings. The many tangled ideas about being harmed, or damaged, or lost, illusions about burglars, and spies among the shadows or in the closet, can all be woven into a special pattern of being punished for wrongdoing. Anything that happens can be interpreted as punishment. . . ."

How Divorce Counseling Can Be Useful

There are times when it may become useful for one or both spouses to obtain psychological counseling for no other reason than to enable them to negotiate their divorce rather than litigate it.

Mr. Brown came to see his lawyer one afternoon. At thirty-six, he was an executive in a small but fast-growing computer services company. He said he and his wife had not been getting along and he had just moved out of the house into an apartment. He said his wife was very bitter. He had spent too much time away from home at night and on trips in his effort to help the new company grow. He had met his wife when he was stationed in England while in the army. She said she felt isolated in a new suburban subdivision and that her isolation had grown more intense with his absences from home. He said that when she grew "quarrelsome," he began to eat his dinner out—usually with a young female assistant who was employed by his company's accountant.

Mr. Brown said his wife was on the warpath. She had found out about the dinner dates and had gone to a lawyer. He thought she was also going to have him followed although he had no idea where she would get the money to pay for all that.

Mr. Brown said he did not know whether his marriage was dead or not. He missed his children very much—especially now that he was no longer living at home. He and his wife had not taken a vacation together in years and hardly talked any more. He said they still had some sex life together, but neither was really interested in the other. He said she was magnifying his dinner dates out of all proportion.

As he and his lawyer talked, it became obvious to the lawyer that the wife was attempting to place the entire blame for the failing marriage on the girl from the accounting firm. It also became clear that she was less interested in keeping the marriage together than he was. (In fact, he finally admitted that she had talked of divorce three years before when she told him she had never loved him.) She had told him she missed her family, resented her role as a young executive's wife and, in fact, resented being *his* wife. She said she had never respected him. He said she had only married him to get away from her family in England. By now, their anger and hurt were too great for either of them to be reasonable.

Mr. Brown's problem was to contain his wife's now out-of-control rage long enough to reach an agreement about alimony, support, custody, visitation and the sale of the house. The agreement and the separation were what she fundamentally wanted anyway. Her impulsive trip to a lawyer and her interest in hiring a detective were protective attempts at outrage. This indignation justified her own sense of guilt for entering into, and now helping to destroy, her marriage. Her guilt-laden choice of expensive and destructive litigation had to be converted into less costly, more informed and constructive channels through counseling before negotiated divorce could be attempted.

The lawyer suggested to Mr. Brown that he try to interest his wife in seeing a marriage counselor. He jumped at the idea. He hoped it might save the marriage. The lawyer quickly told him not to expect too much and that the efforts of the marriage counselor—a psychologist whom the lawyer knew to be skilled and experienced—could only be focused on trying to make each of them understand the problem better. In this way, Mr. Brown would not be locked into the preconception, throughout the consultations, that the marriage had to be saved. Besides, his lawyer pointed out from a wholly practical standpoint, if the marriage counselor gave Mrs. Brown the idea that the only purpose of the consultation was to keep the marriage intact, she might well walk out.

The lawyer explained that even if the counselor were not to be successful in patching up their marriage, there was something to be gained from the conference anyway. His wife might just learn the reasons her marriage was breaking up. She might purge herself of her guilt through this insight, perhaps quickly, or else through a slower process over a period of months, during which she would come slowly to terms with herself, her marriage and her divorce.

Mr. and Mrs. Brown started seeing the psychologist the lawyer had recommended, whom we shall call Dr. MacFarland. Dr. MacFarland's method was to see the husband and wife at the same time. In the case of the Browns, this made sense, particularly in view of their modest means. He charged $25 an hour; his rate was the same whether one or both were present. After a month of sessions—and some thinking in between—Mrs. Brown apparently faced the truth behind their collapsing marriage. Her bitterness abated.

She realized that her husband's offer to pay her $500 a month as well as half the proceeds from the sale of their house was not only reasonable, but also would free her from the expense of a courtroom war and detectives' bills.

After the sessions had terminated, Dr. MacFarland wrote the lawyer:

> I saw them together and once separately. Both want out more than continuing the marriage, with Mr. Brown more ambivalent than Mrs. Brown. He said: "Emotionally I would like the marriage, but *know* it can't continue, in this way."

Both together and alone they recognized the handicapping backgrounds they had brought to the marriage, the impossible demands they had made of one another for ten years and the accumulated pain they felt hopeless to redress and wanted to be free of.

Notwithstanding this insight they each declined an opportunity to explore their problems further to the end that they would have a more solid basis for their decision about the marriage and as an insurance against repeating their problems.

In a sense they saw me to avoid future recriminations but in the process got an overview about what they were responsible for in the failure. This should make it easier for them to take corrective help in the future, but meanwhile, as Mrs. Brown said: "I have to see what I can do with time and experience."

Through these consultations with Dr. MacFarland, Mr. and Mrs. Brown became capable of communication with each other to the end that they could negotiate a reasonable separation and property settlement agreement without the recrimination, fear and disabling emotional tension. Dr. MacFarland operated successfully as a "Divorce Counselor."

The Odds Are That Your Divorce Will Be "Counseled"

Meaningful statistics do not exist on the chances of your ending up married rather than divorced if you consult a "Divorce Counselor." There is no central place for the reporting of results of marriage counseling. Even if there were, the statistics would probably mislead. When a husband or wife consults a psychiatrist about a problem, is that marriage counseling? When warring spouses are interviewed by the judge in a pre-trial conference before the trial, is that marriage counseling?

THE DIVORCE COUNSELORS

Every year a million people are involved and millions more significantly affected by the decisions of a couple to break up: each year's crop of divorces also involves 600,000 children, and all the relatives, employers, lawyers and counselors—religious, social and psychological. Every one of them has a stake in making the process of divorce as civilized, uncomplicated, unemotional, painless, unfrightening and inexpensive as possible.

Divorce itself is now acceptable and accepted. The social process is no longer committed to keeping unwilling husbands and wives together. And, for thousands of those who each year are touched by this new attitude, "divorce counseling" has been an indispensable part of the process of negotiated divorce.

Perhaps it can be for you as well.

[3]

MARITAL MISCONDUCT: THE OLDEST BARGAINING LEVER

You and I can look through all the statutes on divorce and still not find "negotiated divorce" clearly set out by chapter and verse. Instead, you would still see the old-fashioned requirement that there be "grounds" for divorce. Most state statutes still require that before a divorce can be obtained, one spouse must be guilty of "misconduct": that is, one spouse must be proven to be "cruel," or a deserter, or an adulterer. And, even in those sixteen states where misconduct is no longer a requirement for getting a divorce, misconduct, for the most part, can still affect the amount of alimony and child support that must be paid, and who is the better custodian of the children, as well as how husband and wife divide their property. Therefore, even for the husbands and wives who want to negotiate their divorce, marital misconduct is still an important aspect of negotiated divorce.

Most judges are businesslike about their approach to deciding financial questions. Still, many divorce negotiators cannot help but speculate that if they are unable to reach a compromise, a judge—when the unsettled case reaches court—might let his emotions become a factor in the award.

Likewise, too many spouses are willing to subordinate the welfare of the children to their emotional attempts to prove blame, hoping that perhaps the judge will be swayed.

Most Americans who seek a divorce still face the prospect of having to ask their spouse for permission to divorce because, otherwise, they will have no grounds for divorce. If the spouse refuses to grant permission, there often ensue days—or perhaps years—of emotional harangues, in and out of court, over who is at fault, who committed the marital "crime" of walking out first, who could not take the emotional pressure and who hit whom first, and how much—in dollars and cents—each really wants to pay for freedom.

So, *marital misconduct* is often a *key bargaining lever* for obtaining a better property settlement agreement and perhaps even the divorce itself. While some states are trying to eliminate the need for misconduct altogether in granting divorces* and one state (California) has even tried to eliminate misconduct from most financial and custody decisions, evidence of misconduct is still important for most negotiations.

Sometimes the misconduct is obvious and easy to prove. The husband, without his wife's consent or cause, has moved to a bachelor apartment: he has deserted. The wife has started living

*See discussion of "living apart" as a ground for divorce (now adopted in sixteen states), later in this chapter.

with a gigolo and has an illegitimate child to prove it: she is an adulteress. But often sexual misconduct is harder to prove. Here is where a private detective can be helpful.

The Value of a Private Detective

What you need from a private detective is "hard evidence," not just a hint of suspicion. For example, he need not catch your husband *in flagrante delicto* with another woman, but where evidence of adultery is what you are seeking, he must provide you with evidence of your husband's "adulterous opportunity" and "adulterous disposition."* Merely having dinner in a public restaurant with someone of the opposite sex, for example, is wishful thinking. Holding hands while entering a hotel room for the night is regarded as good evidence. Holding hands in a public restaurant, as such, is not. A kiss is pretty good evidence. A hug may not be.

Hiring Detectives Can Bring Unwanted Results

It is important to remember that detectives are not always necessary to today's divorce process and that there are times when employing them may not only constitute a waste of money but can actually *harm* your case. For example, if your wife already feels guilty over her adultery or other misconduct toward you—whether or not you have had proof—you may exploit that guilt during the negotiations by less provocative methods than having her followed day and night. Indeed, she may become so outraged

*An "adulterous opportunity" generally means his being in a darkened room with a lady not his wife. This should happen late at night. Love in the afternoon is harder to prove.

at being subjected to a Tom and Jerry chase that her anger may overcome her guilt—actually making her far more difficult to deal with.

Or, your husband may be in the real estate business, for example, and may have amassed title to lands and buildings which he placed in both your names. You may learn, depending on the state in which you live, that if he wants a divorce or separation agreement, he will have to pay you handsomely for your interest in his real estate—*whether or not he has committed adultery.* He may be more amenable to a generous settlement if you have not provoked him to guilty rage.

Private detectives and sexual misconduct have roles to play in negotiating a divorce, but they are volatile elements which must be handled carefully with the help of a lawyer. They must be used prudently if they are not to be turned against the user.

In hiring a detective, you must be prepared to learn things about your spouse that you may wish you had never known. On the other hand, hiring a detective can have a happy ending too.

Not long ago there was a case of an attractive but domineering wife who suspected that her husband had a girl friend, and hired detectives. The wife was hurt. But she was also mystified.

For years, she had tried to interest her husband in sexual activity with little success. She believed his capacity for sex was dead. But now she learned—from motel receipts again—that his sexual instincts were quite alive.

One night, the detectives followed her husband and his girl friend to a deserted suburban shopping center parking lot. There they saw that the couple was making love in the front seat of their car. When the wife read the details of the parking lot love scene in the detectives' surveillance report, she was both astounded and indignant. She was also impressed.

She had not dreamed that her husband either had the will or knew the way any more. She thought he had become permanently impotent. Now, she realized that his impotence was limited only to her. She went through some self-analysis in which she wondered if it was not her overpowering approach to love-making that had crushed him. She revised her tactics and became, instead, deliberately seductive, intent on getting her husband back into her bed instead of into his car with some other woman. As of this writing, they are still married.

Use the Detective as a Part of the Bargaining Process, Not as a Substitute for It

The best way to obtain the services of a detective is to have your lawyer hire him for you. Having dealt with numerous divorce cases before you walked into his office, your lawyer will know which sleuths are reliable and which are not, and will have a better idea of just how intensive an investigation is necessary.

The services of a detective will cost you, generally speaking, between $10 and $15 an hour, plus expenses. Sometimes, detectives will take a divorce case for a flat fee and continue to work until the needed evidence is obtained. The flat fee can range between $500 and $1,000. Unless you already know a lot about your spouse's habits of infidelity and can guide the detective to the right place at the right time, you might be better off having the detective on a "flat fee" basis. Again, your lawyer can advise you.

Usually, you should not hire a detective before you retain your lawyer. If you do, you may lose the advantage of your attorney's expertise.* For if you really want to negotiate your divorce—out of court—your lawyer must be able, from the moment the detective is hired, to make full use, at the bargaining table, of the evidence uncovered.

Your lawyer can make the point tellingly—out of court—by showing a detective's surveillance report to your spouse's attorney. He will know from the report just what can and cannot be proved. And he can reduce to a dollars-and-cents equivalent the valuation a moralistic judge is apt to place upon the conduct of the erring spouse—should the case go before him and not be settled out of court.

The point is that misconduct—and hiring a detective to prove it—can be a part of the bargaining process—not a substitute for it. Today, evidence of misconduct is only *one* of the bargaining levers in negotiated divorce. Too often it is considered the only lever—with the resultant "messy divorce." It is mentioned here first because it is the best known, although still the most crudely used lever.

"Living Apart": The Light at the End of the Tunnel

If you are lucky enough to live in or near one of the sixteen states** which have "living apart" (or a variation of "living

*For example, your lawyer may suggest that following the suspected girl (or boy) friend may be more beneficial than following your husband (wife).

**By early 1970, the states with "living apart" as a ground for divorce were Alabama (with some statutory modifications), Arkansas, Arizona, California, Idaho, Kentucky, Louisiana, Maryland, North Carolina (although somewhat narrowly interpreted by the courts), South Carolina, Texas, Virginia, Washington, West Virginia, Nevada and Rhode Island (somewhat discretionary with the judge).

apart") as a ground for divorce, you will not have to face hiring detectives to prove "misconduct" in order to get your divorce although you may still need that proof for your private bargaining sessions over money, property, custody and visitation.

"Living apart" is the only ground for divorce which ignores completely any consideration of whether you or your spouse is to blame for the breakdown of your marriage.

All the "living apart" ground asks is whether your marriage has failed and if it has, either you or your spouse can obtain a divorce. The only requirement is that you must live apart from each other for a certain period of time: in some states only a year; in others, up to ten years; in most only two or three years. There is no bargaining about whether there will be a divorce or not. Consent by *both* spouses is *not* necessary. The divorce *must* be granted.

"Living apart" as a ground for divorce is the emancipation proclamation for the spouse whose mate refuses to agree to a divorce. With the widening availability of "living apart" as grounds, any unhappy spouse has the key to divorce in moving out.

But the majority of the states still do not allow "living apart" as a ground for divorce, although, of course, you could go to the trouble of establishing a new residence in a state that recognizes such grounds.*

Those who do not live in or near a "living apart" state must

*Today, for example, the District of Columbia resident can move into Virginia or Maryland, reside the requisite year to establish residence and then, after having lived apart (for two years in Virginia and five years in Maryland), obtain a divorce.

still bargain for a divorce—and marital misconduct is one of the bargaining levers. Still, there are many others—and today a thorough appreciation of the psychological, tax and other bargaining aspects of negotiating a divorce is crucial.

[4]

ALIMONY CAN SAVE A HUSBAND MONEY

A Washington television personality once asked me during her morning interview show: "I've read about all those women who go out to Reno and get huge alimony awards. What advice can you give women to help us get more alimony?"

The answer was simple. I said, "Marry richer men."

Since the interview was being taped, my hostess cut this portion of our interview from the program. The answer did not make very good listening—or so she thought. After all, any wife seeking alimony would not want to hear such a seemingly unhelpful and glib remark. Besides, my answer did not fit in with anything else that is being told men and women each day about how the courts "favor" women in a dispute over alimony, how wives enjoy more power in a divorce fight because they, unlike their husbands, are entitled to have their debtor husbands thrown into jail if they fail to pay alimony.

For that matter, there wasn't anything in my statement particularly comforting to divorcing husbands. I hadn't said that I was opposed to alimony on principle or that alimony was outmoded now that women could and do work.

The fact is that the problem of supporting a wife and children after a divorce cannot be easily solved or described with generalities. So far as I know, the only valid generality is that a husband must support his children—*no matter what.* But (a) *how much* support he must pay for the children and (b) whether or not a husband must *also* support his ex-wife (by paying alimony) depend on many factors:

1. How long has the couple been married?
2. How old are the husband and wife?
3. Are there children? How old are they?
4. How healthy are the husband, wife and children?
5. How able are the husband and wife to earn a living?
6. How much can and do each of them earn?
7. What are the circumstances leading up to the divorce?
8. Is the husband or wife "guilty" of some particularly callous, blatant or offensive misconduct?
9. What was the family's standard of living before the divorce?
10. What will be the needs of the wife and children—and the husband—after the divorce?

The only useful approach to the always troublesome issue of alimony is *not* whether the husband should pay it but *under what circumstances* and how much must he pay.

Alimony, which is financial support for an ex-wife, is not an all or nothing, good or bad, moral or immoral proposition. The process of divorce by negotiation—which emphasizes compromise, relative values and objectivity—is particularly well-suited to provide the answers. Whether or not a husband ends up paying alimony depends on many imprecise points, such as how "blatant" the husband's adultery has been and how "impossible" is it for the wife to work. What better way to resolve these points than a bargaining process in which, slowly but surely, a compromise is struck in which each of many elements plays a part but no one element necessarily controls the whole issue.

In considering the following examples, notice how each time a new element is added, the scales of "justice" tip first one way then the other so that in most cases it would be unfair to give one side all or nothing. Your case may not fall squarely within these examples. Few do. But the principle in each may serve as an important guide.

The Young Marrieds

The first example is relatively easy.

You are a wife in your early twenties. You and your husband probably have only been married a year or two and do not have children. You have been working at the same job since before you were married. Neither you nor your husband has been unfaithful. Both of you have decided that your marriage was a mistake.

Will you want alimony? Not likely. Do you need alimony? No. Would a court order your husband to pay you alimony if you asked for it? Absolutely not. Why? Because you scarcely, if at all, have changed your position by marrying. You have the same job.

You're still young. You still are remarriageable. Since you still have your youth and you have regained your freedom, you should set your sights on *future* opportunities, not *present* problems or *past* mistakes.

The Old Marrieds

This makes the problem a little harder. Assume you are a wife, forty-eight years old. You and your husband have been married for twenty-three years and have two children, now both grown and married. You have not worked since the early years of your marriage. You have forgotten all you ever knew about shorthand and typing. You are totally dependent on your husband for your financial needs. When you study the "Help Wanted" ads in the paper, you see repeated references to "young receptionist"; "computer programmer"; "girl with shorthand speed over 100 words per minute and typing speed over 60 wpm." But you are no longer young, skilled or a girl with any kind of speed. Even if your spirit is willing your flesh will need some re-training.

Let's assume that neither you nor your husband has been unfaithful. Both of you have been waiting for the children to grow up before doing anything about the divorce you have talked about for years. Now the time has come. Do you need alimony?

Yes, for a while anyway, and maybe permanently if you do not remarry.

Will your husband want to pay alimony?

Maybe. But all the years of frustration about his marriage may get in the way of his better judgment. He may blame all the problems of the failed marriage on you. He may see no justification for paying you anything now that the children are grown up. But here is where paying alimony can *save* him money—tax money—and give you the support you need. This is how it works:

Alimony is deductible by husbands on their federal income tax returns (and on most state returns). It is a little help, through tax relief, that the federal government provides to husbands who are divorced. It can save a husband a substantial sum in taxes since his tax rates go up once he is divorced. Remember, he can no longer file a joint income tax return with you and reap the advantages of the lower income tax rates that go along with filing a joint return (that is, unless he remarries).

So, for example, assume your husband has taxable income of $20,000 a year. While he and you were married, he paid taxes in the 32 percent bracket. After he is divorced, he may find himself in as high as the 38 percent bracket. Therefore, if he pays you $200 a month in alimony after the divorce—all of which is deductible on his federal income tax return—he will save up to 38 percent of the $200 or about $70 a month. Because alimony is deductible, paying you $200 a month actually costs your husband about $130 a month after taxes. By paying $2400 a year in alimony, he saves about $840 a year in taxes.

So, it is not surprising that if your husband is in his late forties or fifties he won't object in negotiating to paying you a reasonable amount of alimony, particularly if the proposition is attractively presented to him. Beyond any moral obligation he may feel to take care of you (after all, you are the mother of his children), paying alimony has tax advantages. For a man who is likely to be in his peak earning years, the tax consequences are important.

Now let's take a look at the comparative *Advantages to a Husband and a Wife of Paying Alimony.*

Small Children and Large Needs

Suppose you are a husband who has just found out that your wife has been having an affair. It is the last straw. You have been thinking about divorce for two years but you had concluded that you could endure an imperfect marriage for the sake of the children. Now, however, everyone in your circle must know about your wife's infidelity. You cannot tolerate the mortification: you must have a divorce. Your children are aged seven and nine. You are thirty-seven. Your wife is thirty-five.

Now that your wife has had an affair—and was indiscreet about it—you do not feel any moral obligation to pay her any alimony, like our "old married" husband. You will agree to support the children, but you'll be damned if you'll pay alimony to her.

However, you are quite wrong to take such an emotional view.

Here is where paying alimony can really *save* you large amounts of money. Here is where negotiated divorce gets a real assist from the tax laws.

Here is where two seemingly opposite positions can be reconciled through a tax gimmick.

You can get your divorce, provide support for your children, and obtain tax relief in the bargain. Your wife, who, because of small children, needs support for herself (alimony) as well as for the children, can also get that support for herself provided she pays a little extra in taxes. Here is how it works:

First, let's assume you and your wife fought out your case in court. You would refuse to pay her alimony in light of her adultery. She might sue you to try to get alimony as well as child support. The judge might very well conclude that her adultery has deprived her of the right to alimony. Nevertheless, the judge would still require you to make monthly support payments for the children. Therefore you could win your emotional and moral case but lose the case in your wallet. How?

Payments for child support would be somewhere between 25 percent and 50 percent of your after-tax income. (The more children there are, the closer the amount would come to the 50 percent figure.) So, if you had taxable income of $20,000 a year, your federal and state income taxes after divorce (without the benefit of filing a joint return) could exceed $6500 (instead of the $5700 you had been paying before divorce), leaving you with only $13,500 a year, or $1125 a month, after taxes. Since you have only two children, the judge is apt to require you to pay your wife about one-third of your after-tax income, or $375 a month, all as child support. None of that child support would be deductible. So, you could be left with only $750 a month to live on after you paid taxes and child support.

Now, suppose instead of going to court, you negotiated your divorce—out of court. You could save money.

How? By swallowing your pride and simply agreeing to *allocate,* in the separation agreement, a reasonable portion of the monthly payments to the alimony category.

Why? Because alimony payments are deductible by the husband on his income tax return while child support payments are not.

If you allocated $200 of the $375 monthly payment to the alimony category, you would be able to take a $2400 deduction each year on your federal income tax return. Since you will be in about the 38 percent bracket after divorce, you will be able to save about $840 a year, or about $70 a month. Thus, you would have $820 a month in your pocket after paying taxes and alimony and support instead of $750 a month.

ALIMONY CAN SAVE A HUSBAND MONEY

There is still another reason why it makes good sense for a husband to agree to label a portion of the monthly payment as alimony: You can automatically stop sending alimony payments to your ex-wife when she remarries. Considering that eight out of ten divorced women remarry, the odds of such a break are in your favor. If your wife were to remarry, you will get a $100 a month wedding present *from her* in the form of an automatic reduction in this amount each month in the check you must send her.*

In some cases it is possible and even advantageous for the husband to deduct his entire support package. The United States Supreme Court has ruled (in the case of the television comedian, Jerry Lester) that *all* of the money a husband pays is alimony and deductible by him on his tax return if he makes no specific allocation but obligates himself to support his ex-wife and children. On the other hand, the wife must pay income tax on all of the support money she receives from her husband. Careful legal and accounting counseling and drafting are required when using the Lester Rule, but it can be valuable, especially to husbands in the higher income tax brackets who find difficulty in supporting themselves, ex-wives and children, and the United States Treasury in the manner to which all have been accustomed.

The husband assumes some risks when he allocates a portion of the child support payments to alimony, which must be weighed along with the advantages.

Your ex-wife may not remarry. When the husband agrees to pay alimony, he is gambling on his wife's remarriage. If she does not remarry, he will be stuck with making alimony payments for

*If your ex-wife is independently rich, it still might pay, from a tax point of view, to allocate some of the child support to alimony. This would particularly pay off if and when your ex-wife remarries.

the rest of her life, that is, even after the children have grown up and he is no longer obligated to support them.

The Internal Revenue Service may be less generous. If *too great* a portion of the child support payments are allocated to alimony, the Internal Revenue Service will disallow all or a portion of the deduction the husband takes for alimony as unreasonable when compared to the number of children he also supports.

The wife may love the alimony check more than remarriage. By allocating too much of the monthly payment to alimony, the husband may deter his ex-wife from remarrying. Many a woman has hesitated before giving up a certain fat alimony payment in return for the uncertain promises of a new suitor.

In general, wisely counseled husbands often prefer paying alimony to their ex-wives especially when they have to support young children. They will have to support them until they grow up anyway (usually until age twenty-one), so why not get some tax relief? Why not let Uncle Sam help with the support payments?

Whenever you negotiate, you must always think of the "other side" and how she is likely to react to what you are saying. So, here is what she is likely to be thinking when you are talking about alimony.

There are also advantages to the wife in receiving alimony.

She is likely to get more money. When a husband makes a tax saving he is more receptive to the argument that he should share some of that saved money with you.

She will receive some income in her old age. While child support payments end when the children reach age twenty-one, alimony goes on. Customarily, alimony must be paid so long as the wife is alive and has not remarried (provided the husband is alive too).

So, alimony can be the old-age pension for an unmarried ex-wife.

Along with these advantages, *there are also disadvantages to the wife in getting alimony.*

She will have to pay more in taxes. Since the wife must pay income tax on alimony she receives but no income tax on child support she receives, the wife assumes an additional tax obligation when she agrees to receive alimony. If alimony is the only taxable income she receives, her tax rate is likely to be low enough to minimize this problem. But, if she decides to go to work and earn $5000 or more, this further income, together with her alimony income, can push her into a surprisingly uncomfortable, high income tax bracket.

If you are a divorcing wife, you must carefully calculate the tax consequences of accepting alimony. Moreover, if possible, you should bargain with your husband for a little extra alimony to cover the tax obligation that goes along with the alimony you are about to receive. If your husband will not agree to help with the extra tax burden you assume when you receive alimony, you should carefully consider whether or not you might not be better off allocating the entire monthly check from your husband to child support.

She will usually lose all alimony when she remarries. The wife must sit back and calculate coolly whether she is apt to remarry and how soon. (Of course, if you are getting divorced for the express purpose of marrying someone else, then you surely don't want any alimony.) In assessing your position, you must carefully weigh your age, number of children and their ages, your attractiveness and your sexual resiliency. If, after such an assessment, you conclude that you are likely to remarry and soon, don't allocate much, if anything, to alimony because alimony ends on your remarriage.

To be sure, each consideration in paying or accepting alimony must be balanced by the husband and wife along with all of the other issues facing them as they negotiate their divorce and separation agreement. Those issues and how they are best negotiated will be discussed in the next two chapters.

[5]

THE NEGOTIATING WIFE: BETTER A BARGAINER THAN A BLACKMAILER BE

What should a wife know in order to better prepare herself and her lawyer to negotiate her divorce? Here are some of the most important points:

Remember Who "The Opposition" Is

You should not begin the bargaining process by calling your husband a cad and an adulterer, or the sole cause of the breakdown of your marriage. You should not remind him of the times when he has been unfair, irresponsible and ungenerous. Instead, you should remind him of the needs of the minor children, assuming there are any, and *his* hopes for *their* future. You should not start by enshrouding the negotiations in an adversary climate.* You should not threaten to "take every last cent he's got," to drag him into court, to expose his shortcomings or his mistakes.

If you threaten to expose, if you start with blackmail in your heart, you are most likely to encounter more of the same from your husband, or worse, to find he is reluctant to negotiate at all. He will be afraid to offer you a fair and reasonable settlement, fearing you are so bitter that you will only reject his offer and demand more. In fact, you may never receive his best offer because you have made him fearful or too aggravated.

You may argue that you know your husband better and that he will never voluntarily be reasonable and generous. If you are right, then there is always time to threaten or to sue. But rarely is anything lost by trying to be reasonable at first. You just may find, to your surprise, that like most women who negotiate their divorces, your offers of reasonableness will be met by the same from him.

The opposition is your husband, not "the enemy." In all probability, you were once in love with him. He still is the father of your children. He may yet be a friend to your parents if not to you as well. He will probably be an important—if not *the* most

*Lawyers should remember this too. When a wife's lawyer writes a letter to the husband's lawyer, for example, he should *not* have his secretary type "*Jones versus Jones*" at the top of each page. The case is not "versus" yet. It can still be simply a "matter of the Jones Family" or just "Jones." After all, when the husband's lawyer receives it, he should—and probably will in this day of Xerox machines—make a copy of the wife's lawyer's letter and send it to the husband. It will not help the negotiating climate to dramatize the conflict that lurks just beneath the quiet bargaining surface. Likewise, a lawyer should hesitate before he flays the other spouse with a letter of accusation and recrimination. Such stern talk can better be used in person or by telephone—between the lawyers, who have a better capacity to forget. Once it is in writing it often takes on an air of permanence and importance which probably far exceeds the intentions of the writer at the time. In short, don't put the recriminations in writing.

important—source of your income for years to come. He has an obligation to support the children—and perhaps you too. But whether he lives up to his obligation reliably and on time can make a big difference to you in years to come. And how you treat him at the time of the divorce can have a lasting effect on whether he lives up to that obligation and whether he does so voluntarily.

Thus, you should start the negotiations by appealing to your husband's sense of fairness.

You should also appeal to his sense of responsibility to his children, if not to you too. You should appeal to his disposition —however now repressed—to be generous to them, if not to you as well. A husband—even if he becomes an ex-husband—generally does not want to see his children poorly cared for or denied the opportunity to enter college. At the time of divorce, most husbands still hope that they will be able to maintain a decent relationship with their children. Divorce is the time for you to capitalize on your husband's hopes, by securing a generous support payment for the children—and indirectly for you too—as well as his promise to pay for their college education.

Decide Who Should Negotiate—You or Your Lawyer

If you have never been able to keep up with your husband's financial discussions or explanations, you should not start now. If your husband has always lectured to you on matters of money, now is the time to put an end to those lectures. His offers may be generous and reasonable. But you should let your lawyer find that out first. Your lawyer is far less likely to be taken advantage of. He will know whether your husband is being truthful when he reveals his income and his assets. Whether you understand financial matters or not, you are better off letting your lawyer negotiate for you. You can still talk to your husband, and listen to his arguments and problems. You need not be rude or cut him off. You can simply refer any proposals or requests to your lawyer. The reason is simple—you are far too emotionally involved in your problem to be able to react instantly, objectively and advantageously. You have too much at stake to represent yourself.

There is one exception to this rule. There are wives who are able to "handle" their husbands. They have not only kept all the financial records, paid the bills and prepared the income tax returns but they have also been able to assert their will over their husbands in most family affairs. For them, a divorce is not the time to stop "handling" things. Many a charming or tough-minded wife has been able to gain more than her lawyer ever could by engaging in face-to-face bargaining with her husband while her lawyer counsels patiently from the sidelines.

Examine Your Budget Carefully

We will examine in Chapter 7 the list of items the wife should include in her budget. You should study that list. Some of the items discussed below, however, are less obvious than others and are often lost in the heat—or coolness—of the negotiations. That forgetfulness may then come back to haunt you. So, I discuss them here to give them special emphasis.

[Remarriage Equipment]

A post-divorce vacation, cosmetics, beauty parlor, magazines, books, club dues, theater and movies, other types of entertainment (including expenses for extra food and drink for parties) are important for most women. But for a woman who is divorced, they are more than important. They are necessities of life. They are her "remarriage equipment."

Your husband may regard these as frill items or too large. But you should have your lawyer point out to him that if he were to examine the family's budget while you and he were living together, he would agree that these "extras" were often as major an element in his budget as the old-fashioned necessities of life such as food, shelter and clothing. He may argue that he is not responsible for his ex-wife's entertainment, or for the maintenance of her beauty. But it should be pointed out to him that he is wrong and not for reasons that merely benefit you: remarriage equipment is an investment in his potential release from alimony.

An entertainment allowance and beauty aids will reveal you in an attractive light to prospective new husbands. Your lawyer should remind your husband that if he bargains wisely and allocates a portion of the child support to the alimony category, then he will have a special interest in your remarriage. Remember, if you remarry, that portion of the monthly payment allocated to alimony for you automatically stops.

[Don't Forget to Include an Income Tax Allowance in Your Budget]

While we are talking about alimony, you should not forget that you must pay income tax on that portion of the monthly check that is allocated to alimony in the separation agreement. You can prepare yourself to pay this additional expense by bargaining for a little extra in the monthly alimony and support check to cover the extra expense you have assumed by agreeing to receive alimony. After all, if you have helped your husband to obtain tax relief, the least your husband can do, you can argue, is to reimburse you for the extra income tax liability you have incurred.

[If Alimony Can Save a Husband Money, He Should Share Some of Those Savings with You]

Now, let us go one more logical step further in your negotiations with your husband. In Chapter 4, we discussed how a husband can save money by allocating some of the monthly support for the children to the alimony category. We explained how you should be reimbursed for the extra tax expense you incur by agreeing to receive alimony. But you can also take the position that you should receive something more in return for the tax saving you have agreed to provide.

Here are some arguments that can be used effectively:

1. You need almost the same amount of money to support the children as you do to support the children and yourself. The children's food budget is not greatly increased by adding one more mouth—yours—to the list of people who eat from that budget. The size of the apartment you must rent or the house you must purchase is not greatly increased by adding one more person to its occupants. Therefore, the monthly check for the children will be virtually the same whether you are considered to be fed and clothed by it or not. (If your husband should argue that some of the money he pays must be benefiting you directly, then you or your lawyer can retort that any benefit you receive is more than offset by the services you furnish free of charge when you take care of the children. After all, who else will cook and clean for his children as cheaply?)

2. So, if your husband is actually paying little extra for your

support, while at the same time you are permitting him to allocate some of the child support payment to alimony so that he can save income tax, then the least he can do is pay you a little more each month—preferably in nontaxable child support—in return for the tax favor.

[New Car and New Furniture]

You should not forget that you will need to buy a new car at least every three or four years, unless you are prepared to pay costly repair bills. Likewise, you will need to replace furniture as it wears out. Monthly alimony and support checks rarely provide enough to cover replacing these large items—and they should.

Keep Your Own Earnings for Your Own Rainy Day

Sooner or later in the negotiations, your husband will claim that if you are going to earn money by working, then he should get a reduction in alimony and child support. At first, this seems like a reasonable argument. After all, if you have been reasonable in your approach to him, then you have been emphasizing that you only want enough for what you actually need for yourself and the children. Therefore, when you earn your own income, it could reasonably be argued that your need for his money should decrease. But there is a fallacy in the husband's argument because what he will pay in alimony and child support covers much less than he thinks. Over the years, inflation tends to deflate alimony checks. Particularly good examples of expenses rarely covered by alimony and support payments are those items which wear out and which the divorced wife must replace: the washing machine, the television set, rugs, furniture, etc.

The whole concept of alimony and support payments is based on day-to-day needs of the wife and children. Somehow, monthly payments never cover the big-ticket items that need replacement. Therefore, your own earnings will become indispensable sources for satisfying these needs. In addition, there are vacations and summer camps and piano lessons for the children. The list can go on and on.

Lastly, you can argue that your husband should not look too greedily at the money you earn because, after all, you will have many expenses to meet before you can call your salary your own. First of all, income tax and social security contributions are withheld. Then you must buy clothes to go to work in, pay carfare or tolls to get there or parking fees when you arrive, and perhaps employ a baby sitter while you are away. Therefore, even if your husband insists on receiving a credit for your earnings, he will find your *net* earnings are relatively small.

Own a House; Don't Pay Rent

You should negotiate to obtain title to the house you and your husband were purchasing before the divorce. And, if you and your husband were not purchasing a house before the divorce, you should try to buy one after the divorce.

This may seem like presumptuous advice. After all, if you could afford to buy a house, you think, surely you would. But there are special reasons for emphasizing the importance to a divorced woman of owning her own home.

Getting a divorce is often a frightening experience. And nowhere is the fright greater than in the financial area. You are cutting your ties to your husband. You are casting yourself adrift, often far away from the great rock of your financial stability. Even if your husband was not a great provider in the past, he was, nevertheless, the major breadwinner. Now with the divorce, you and the children are losing your *automatic* claim to his support. You can do much, in the separation agreement, to tie him to you and the children financially, but it is still only an agreement, and it can be broken. Then, all you can do is sue him. Besides, he can die and all you will have is the proceeds of his life insurance (if you have been a careful negotiator).

So, to a large extent, much of your security must come from yourself—or at least through your own financial planning. Even a wife who cannot, or does not, work because of her desire to stay home and care for her small children, can do much to provide for her own financial security. And one of the most important things she can do is spend part of the alimony and support *not* on rent but on purchasing a house.

With every mortgage payment you make, you are gradually making the house your own. Even if you later sell it, you will discover that you have saved thousands of dollars. Here is how it works:

You and your husband decide to sell your house, which is now too large (or too costly) for your new circumstances, and discover that you can get $38,000 for it. You still owe $26,000 on the mortgage. You must pay about $2000 in salesman's commission. But after all that is taken care of, you and your husband should receive a check for about $10,000.

Let us assume that you and your husband agree to divide equally the $10,000 you have received from the sale of the house.

You can take your $5,000 and probably purchase a $25,000

house. You can borrow the other $20,000 from a bank. Your mortgage payments will approximate $155 a month, and your real estate taxes and utilities will approximate another $75 a month (depending on the area of the country you live in and the condition of the house). But, of the $230 a month you are paying in mortgage, taxes and utilities for your house, you will probably save $35 a month. Save? Yes, save, because at least $35 of your mortgage payment goes to pay off the mortgage loan itself (the rest goes for interest). That means you will save $420 a year.

If you never move, by the time the children grow up and your husband stops sending you support payments for them, you will not need as much each month because your house will have been paid for.

If you do move and sell your house, you will discover that you have saved at least $420 a year, plus the amount of money your house has increased in value, especially due to inflation.

There are additional advantages to a divorced wife that accrue from buying a home rather than renting an apartment. In addition to the sense of security that comes from owning your own home and from building a nest egg, there are substantial tax benefits.

As a homeowner, you can deduct the interest payments and real estate taxes on your income tax return. Let us assume that your husband will pay you $500 a month in alimony and support with $250 of it allocated as alimony. You must pay income tax on the portion that is allocated as alimony. That means that even if you have no income other than the alimony, you will still have to pay taxes on $250 a month or $3,000 a year.

You cannot take the children as exemptions on your income tax return because your husband is the one who is providing more than half—if not all—of their financial support. So, after taking yourself as a dependent (a total of $650 in deductions*), there is little else to deduct. The tax on the remaining $2350 a year (or on the remaining $2000 a year, if you have a few deductions such as charity to lower your taxable income) will be about $425 in federal and state income taxes.

But, if you can deduct the interest and real estate taxes you pay for your house, you will hardly have to pay *any* income taxes. The interest payments on the house mortgage approximate $120 a month or $1440 a year. The real estate taxes are another $500. These $1940 in deductions reduce the amount of income on which you have to pay tax from $2000 to $60—thus reducing the taxes from $425 to less than $10.

Therefore, you can save about $415 a year in income taxes (or about $35 a month in extra income). The $230 expense of paying for a house (and its taxes and utilities) is therefore reduced by $35 in savings (from paying off the mortgage) and $35 in income tax savings. Thus, your house expense is reduced effectively from $230 a month to $160 a month.

There is one risk to buying a home: it may land you in a barren husband-hunting area. But today's sexual climate—even in suburbia—is far more receptive to a divorced woman: your neighbors may be able to introduce you to eligible men. Also, there are "Parents Without Partners" clubs throughout the country. You will have to weigh the advantages of one neighborhood over another. But, if it can be done, you should bargain for the house or for enough cash to make a down payment on a new house.

*In 1972, the per person exemption will increase to $700; in 1973 and thereafter, to $750.

Try to Write an Escalation Clause into the Separation Agreement

From the point of view of the wife, an escalation clause in the settlement agreement is a great advantage. An escalation clause automatically increases alimony and child support as your ex-husband's income increases. The advantage of an escalation clause is its *automatic* operation. If your ex-husband earns more, you and the children automatically receive more alimony and support. You will not have to ask your ex-husband for more alimony and child support, and if he refuses, you will not have to pay a lawyer to go to court to ask the judge to order him to pay more.

It is true that the laws of all states always allow a wife to seek an increase (or the husband a decrease) in the amount of child support she receives. (And the laws of many states—but not all—also allow the wife to seek an increase in alimony for herself.) A mother is always allowed to show that her circumstances have changed and that she needs more for the children.*

Nevertheless, a wife should never underestimate the burden of going to court to obtain an increase in child support or alimony. Besides the additional legal fees, the burden rests on her to prove that her needs are greater and that her ex-husband has the increased ability to meet them.

True, your needs and those of your children will increase as they get older and the cost of living rises. But, by then, your ex-husband may have a new wife and more children and, while that is unfortunate, that is also "life." A judge may be sympathetic to your increased needs but he is also apt to tell you that

*Some states also permit a mother to gain an increase in child support merely because the father has increased his income, whether or not the children actually *need* more money.

you "cannot get blood from a turnip." So, the automatic increase provision of an escalation clause in a separation agreement avoids many problems in the future.

An escalation clause provides that the ex-husband shall pay the ex-wife, as increased alimony and child support, or both, a certain percentage of that portion of his income (after taxes) which exceeds the income he was earning at the time the separation agreement was negotiated.

For example, your husband may agree to pay you $500 a month in alimony and child support at a time when he is earning $14,000 a year (or about $11,000 after taxes). He may realize it will be hard for you and the children to get along on $500 a month but due to the size of his earnings, he just cannot pay more. You would be wise, therefore, to bargain for an escalation clause providing that, for each additional $1000 of income he earns each year (after taxes) over $14,000 he shall pay you and the children an additional $250 a year (25 percent) or about $20 a month.

The increased payments would begin with May 1 of the year following the year in which your husband earned the increased income. (Why May? Because your husband has to have time to complete his income tax returns and as part of the agreement must supply a copy of them to you.)

In the example above, you received a quarter of each additional $1000 your husband earned *after* taxes. While 25 percent may not appear to be a high percentage, you should not discourage him from increasing his earnings; otherwise he may not increase them at all, or, if he does, he is likely to attempt to hide the increase. The increased payments are then allocated between alimony and child support in the same ratio as the original alimony and child support payments were allocated.

Don't Be Greedy

Surprising though it may be, you may find that your husband is willing to provide more than he can possibly afford. Many a husband—struggling with oversized feelings of guilt about his failing marriage and the innocent children who have been hurt as a result—will offer to pay more alimony and support than he can prudently afford.

If your husband obligates himself—either willingly or reluctantly—to pay more than he can afford, sooner or later he will be unable to make those payments and will begin to fall behind or to reduce them.

At first, you may be able to overlook the fact that the payments have become reduced or late, but if the reductions or delays continue you may be unable to tolerate them. Yet you will have a hard time collecting the arrears (the name lawyers give to unpaid alimony and support payments), because your ex-husband just will not have the money to pay them. Lawsuits are inherently expensive and likely to be futile. Moreover, if you can completely trap yourself through your greed, you may even try to have your husband thrown in jail for "non-support," thereby completing the full cycle—from over-generosity to no support at all.

Looking for the Lump Sum

What if there are no children to support and your husband hesitates to pay alimony? Or, what if you have children but your husband still hesitates to pay alimony, despite the tax advantages to him? Or, what if your husband is willing to pay you alimony but you are planning a quick remarriage which would automatically terminate all alimony?

There is a solution to each of these problems. It is a lump sum settlement by the husband to the wife. Your husband can pay you all of the lump sum at the time you sign an agreement, or he can pay it in installments. The lump sum settlement is *not* deductible by the husband on his income tax return nor need the wife pay income tax on the lump sum (unless installments are spread out over more than ten years).

The lump sum has several advantages to you. First of all, it is not called alimony and so its name tends not to frighten your husband. Secondly, it is a one-time payment by the husband and many a man will do anything once. Thirdly, it is a "bird in the hand." You need not worry about collecting the lump sum or returning it when you remarry. It is yours to keep. (No lump sum, no signature. No signature, no easy uncontested divorce.) Fourthly, you pay no tax on the lump sum.

But the lump sum has its disadvantages and impracticalities. Many men just do not have a lump sum in their estate and resent being asked for it, especially if they don't have it. And many a woman, for budgeting purposes, would rather have the payments coming in from their ex-husband on a monthly basis. (Of course, you can always invest the lump sum and have it paid out to you in installments plus interest.) Some women are poor managers and fear they will squander the large check or maybe they are predicting their husband will strike it rich and they want to be able to ask for increases in their alimony checks. (The lump sum payment is *in lieu* of alimony. Usually, once it is received, the wife is forever barred from seeking alimony, although she may still seek child support.)

Keep the Furniture and Furnishings

Most husbands are willing to let the wife keep the furniture and furnishings, especially if there are children. Clearly, the initial needs of his wife and children are greater than his. She has more bedrooms to furnish and needs more dining room chairs and kitchen utensils and equipment.

Since it often takes years to accumulate furniture and furnishings, you should not underestimate the cost of their replacement. While he may not have needed them anyway, a husband who relinquishes all claim to furniture and furnishings has really given you a benefit worth remembering during the negotiations.

Hospital and Medical Bills

Separation agreements vary in their approach to the problem of who pays the hospital and medical bills of the wife and children after divorce.

a. The oldest and least satisfactory method is simply to require that the wife pay all medical and hospital bills out of the monthly alimony and support check.

The problem with this approach is that the husband or the wife are seldom able to predict just what hospital and medical expenses the family is likely to incur. If the wife's estimate is too high, the husband will accuse her of padding her demands for support and alimony; if she estimates too low, she may be in trouble later.

b. As a reaction to the problem inherent in the wife having to predict hospital and medical expenses, some husbands and wives have gone to the other extreme. They have agreed that all medical and hospital bills for the children (and for the wife, until she remarries) will be paid by the husband. While this may sound all right from the wife's point of view, experience with this arrangement indicates that it tends to irritate both parties. The husband often regards the unexpected medical bill as unnecessary—particularly if the child turns out not to have been very sick. He may accuse the wife of being a hypochondriac and refuse to pay the bill. If the agreement has obligated the husband to pay drug bills, he may accuse the wife of inserting non-drug items in the pharmacy bills. Problems caused by little bills tend to create a climate of ill will which often makes more serious problems, such as custody and visitation rights, difficult to handle.

c. A better approach is a compromise.

1. Obligate yourself to pay, say, the first $250 of medical, hospital and medicine bills for the children (and for yourself, until you remarry), in any one calendar year, and your husband should agree to pay any bills over $250 a year. To protect yourself, include an item of $20 to $25 in your monthly budget when you commence to bargain for alimony and support.

2. Require your husband to maintain a major medical insurance policy for himself and the children which should cover most bills over $250 a year.

3. Since your husband usually cannot include his ex-wife in his major medical insurance coverage, he or you should take out a separate policy for you. (The better approach would be for you to take out a policy for yourself, particularly if you obtain employment from an employer who offers health insurance. Since the employer often will deduct a portion of the premium for this insurance from your salary, this will help you to convince your husband that he should receive no direct benefit—such as decreased alimony or support allotments—from your separate earnings.)

Require Insurance on Your Husband's Life

Most separation agreements provide that the husband's obligation to support the wife and children ends when the husband dies. Even if agreements provided that the husband's estate must continue to make the alimony and support payments after he died, there is a good chance that there will not be enough money in the estate to honor this obligation.

Today's separation agreements regularly meet this problem by requiring the husband to maintain life insurance on his life with the wife and children as beneficiaries. With some skillful drafting, the premiums can even be made deductible by the husband on his income tax return—a further incentive to the husband to take out plenty of life insurance.

If your husband should object to naming you as beneficiary, you should suggest that he name the children as beneficiaries with you as trustee to hold the insurance proceeds for their benefit. (Since you will have to support the children after he is gone, you should have control over the life insurance proceeds without interference from others.)

How much life insurance should you bargain for? The answer depends on how much your husband can afford, how much alimony and support he is paying and the ages and health of the children and wife. Agreements customarily provide for life insurance payments ranging from $10,000 to hundreds of thousands of dollars.

You should write safeguards concerning the life insurance into the agreement.

a. Your husband should send you written confirmation from the insurance companies involved indicating that the insurance companies are agreeable to those provisions of the separation agreement which forbid him to borrow against the policies or to change the beneficiaries until, for example, the children are graduated from college or, if they already have been graduated, until you have died or remarried.

b. Your husband, each year, should send you bills indicating that the premiums have been paid. If he fails to make the payment, you should have the right to pay the unpaid premium and to compel him to reimburse you for your expense as if it were an arrearage in alimony and support.

Custody and Visitation Rights

If you fail to negotiate your divorce and the separation agreement, the chances are it is because you could not agree on what to do about the children. The reason is obvious. It is much easier to compromise about money than the future well-being of the children.

If the actual *safety* and *welfare* of your children are truly the issue, compromise and bargaining about that may be—and perhaps should be—rejected. If your husband regards you as an unfit mother, if, as evidence, he cites the fact that you fill the household daily—or nightly—with lovers, exposing your children to confusion, uncertainty and a distorted view of sex, or if there is evidence that you are an alcoholic and beat your children when you are drunk, or that you are mentally ill and endanger your home with the fires from forgotten cigarettes, you should not expect your husband to be willing to agree to your having unfettered custody of the children.

But such situations fall within the 10 percent of the divorces that are left to the judges to decide. The other 90 percent of today's divorces—and provisions for custody of the children involved—are negotiated out of court. How?

In almost every case of negotiated divorce, the wife assumes custody of the children. They live with her most, if not all, of the week, and most, if not all, months of the year. Rarely does a case of negotiated divorce result in the husband assuming custody of the children. If he does, it is usually as a result of the mother voluntarily relinquishing her claim to the children either because she wants to be a free soul, or because of her sexual promiscuity or mental illness, or because she recognizes that for various reasons, she could not possibly convince a judge that the welfare of the children lies with their living with her.

Assuming that, as in most cases, you as the wife are the one to have custody, the most troublesome issue that arises in this area will stem from your husband's attempt to preserve his relationship with the children after divorce despite his new status as a visiting parent. The approaches to this problem are many, but the three most common ones are what I call "The Reasonableness Approach," "The Distrust Approach" and "The Balanced Visitation Approach."

The Reasonableness Approach

Here, the husband and wife generally feel confident about each other and their relationship to the children. They merely provide in their agreement that "the wife shall have custody of the children and the husband shall have the right to have the children visit with him at mutually agreeable and reasonable times and places, after the husband provides the wife with reasonable notice."

Here, the husband does not fear that the wife, once she has the custody of the children, will prevent his access to them. The wife does not fear that the husband, once he takes the children on visits, will "turn them" against her or keep them longer than she wants him to.

"The Reasonableness Approach" does not specify which days of the week the husband can or cannot visit the children, or what days, holidays or weeks of the year the children will visit with their father. Nor does it specify how much notice the father must give before he plans a visit. The sole guide is the requirement that the husband and wife be reasonable about their arrangements for the children. This plan of reasonableness applies to choosing schools, neighborhoods, colleges, notification of illness and religious training.

This is an arrangement chosen by a majority of the couples who negotiate their divorce. Its virtues are simplicity and flexibility. Its weaknesses can be unpredictability (if the husband or wife, or both, are in fact unreasonable) and disputes (again, if the husband or wife, or both, later become unreasonable).

The particular advantage to the wife of this arrangement is that, since the husband's visiting times are not specifically stated, the wife has a virtual veto over when and whether the husband can visit with the children. Since the wife has possession of the children, she can refuse to permit them to leave the house, or she can refuse to let their father in to see them or to take them out. She should, and usually does, give a reason for her refusal. Once she does, she cloaks her veto with an air of reasonableness which may very well discourage the father from going to court to protest her conduct; and if he does go to court, she is likely to convince the judge that her excuses are reasonable. All in all, "The Reasonableness Approach" gives the wife a lever over the husband.

The Distrust Approach

Here, the divorcing husband and wife have little or no confidence in the other's good conduct toward the children or toward each other. The husband may fear that the wife will create any excuse to prevent him from seeing the children. The wife may fear that the husband will continually harass her with too frequent visits, disrupt the children's routine, entice them with treats and presents and confuse them or upset them and make them difficult to discipline.

To prevent each from abusing the other and the children, either the husband or the wife use "The Distrust Approach." This specifies exactly what days of the week, what hours of the day, what days, holidays or weeks of the year the husband may visit with the children. The amount of detail will depend on the degree each distrusts the other. Sometimes, the holidays during which the husband will have the children with him will be apportioned years in advance or will be arbitrarily divided. (For example, one will have the right to have the children Christmas Eve, the other Christmas Day.)

The advantages to the wife from "The Distrust Approach" are several: She knows exactly when to expect her ex-husband to visit and she can plan accordingly. She can take the position that, since her ex-husband agreed to a specific time and number of visits, he is not entitled to other or more visits unless she agrees. Her veto remains: except that the father has carved out some exceptions to it.

The disadvantages to the mother in "The Distrust Approach" are also several: experience has revealed that husbands tend to feel obligated to visit the children if the times and dates of the visits are specifically set down in writing in advance. The wife who is anxious not to be bothered by her ex-husband's visits may find that, through "The Distrust Approach," she has forced him to become a regular visitor.

The mother will have to consider whether the advantages of "The Distrust Approach" outweigh the disadvantages. Sometimes, if the distrust is really rampant, the agreement will specify more than just visits. It will set out who shall have the ultimate decision about choice of schools or colleges, in what religion the children will be raised, in what city must the mother and children live, who can or cannot be present during the father's visits with the children, and where the father can visit with the children.

The specifics and restrictions often reflect areas of dispute during the marriage or events leading up to the divorce. For example, a husband will be forbidden from visiting with his children in the presence of women friends if his adultery has been a factor in the marriage or divorce. Or, a wife will be forbidden to move far from the family's former home town if hers has been a history of frustrating the husband's attempts to maintain a close relationship with his children.

Experience has shown, however, that no matter how zealous husbands or wives are, at the time of the divorce, in asserting their rights to visit—or limits on visits—in a majority of cases, divorced husbands gradually grow away from their children. They gradually get used to a new hybrid role of a "sometime visitor" and "partial provider." True, if a husband has had a good relationship with his children before divorce, he tends to have a good relationship with them after divorce. If a husband has done little to perpetuate an intimate relationship with his children before divorce, his relationship is apt to become even less meaningful after divorce (except that, after divorce, he is apt to blame the wife or the lawyers for his failure, citing the restrictive separation agreement or the lawyer who counseled him not to fight for custody).

The Balanced Visitation Arrangement

In most cases, husbands and wives are willing simply to provide that the husband has the right to visit at mutually agreeable reasonable times and places on reasonable notice ("The Reasonableness Approach"). But the mother is apprehensive lest the father "overdo" the visiting (after all, she is no longer his wife and, presumably, does not want to see him more often than she has to). And the father is afraid the mother's new husband may interfere.

For these and other reasons, the best compromise is to provide that "the husband shall have the right to visit with the children at reasonable and mutually agreeable times and places on reasonable notice *including* certain *specified* days of the week or weekends or summer vacations "with any additional times having to be agreed to by both the husband and the wife." By this approach the husband obtains minimum specific visit times (but is not placed in a straitjacket schedule) and the wife has limited the husband (without losing the right to be liberal if she wishes).

You should analyze what your husband's relationship with the children has been before determining what kind of provisions for visits after divorce should be contained in your separation agreement. If your husband has been a five-days-a-week worker and two-days-a-week golfer, you have little cause to worry about his changing his stripes after divorce. You need not fear his sitting on your doorstep. Moreover, if you attempt to restrict his visits, you may find him visiting every hour that he is permitted by the agreement to visit, "just to show you."

If your husband has had an intimate and healthy relationship with the children, you may have a problem with the frequent visits but that needn't be all bad. After all, he is your children's father. In a real sense, your worry about the frequent visits is a "high class worry." His willingness to have the children frequently, his attempts to perpetuate a real relationship with the children—even when separate households make that more difficult—are valuable to the children and may very well be workable into your new routine. In the long run, the children will benefit from his love and attention more than from his disruption of the routine of you and the children. Like all other issues to be negotiated you must weigh both sides and strike the proper balance to meet your particular family's situation.

Your Children's College Education

Most separation agreements contain a provision by which the husband agrees to provide for the college education of the children. However, your husband may want to qualify his obligation by insisting that he only pay "to the extent that he is able" or "to the best of his ability."

The best approach to obtaining a generous provision for your children's college education is to propose that, if your husband agrees to pay all tuition, room, board and miscellaneous expenses of a child at college, you will agree that for each full month that that child is living away from home, your husband can reduce the support payment for that child by at least one-half. You will still need to receive some child support for that child—even while he or she is away at college. You still must clothe him or her and you still must maintain a home for the child to return to at vacation time. Still you can afford to offer a generous reduction in return for his generosity toward them and their education.

There is another aspect to the matter of negotiating for your children's college education: security. Suppose your husband is a good promiser but you wonder if he will deliver when the time comes. After all, he may remarry, or lose his job, or resent his increasing alienation from the children as the years go by.

There are basically two solutions to this problem: (1) You can insist that when the house is sold, your husband's half of the proceeds of sale be placed in a savings account requiring the joint signatures of you and your husband for withdrawals and to be used only for the children's college education. (2) You can provide that your husband pay a sum each month (in addition to alimony and support) into a savings account—also held jointly with you.

The combinations and varieties of arrangements are many. Your lawyer will be able to guide you. The major limit to his ingenuity will be your willingness to accept his guidance and the willingness of your husband and his lawyer to cooperate. The keys to success are careful thought, patience and flexibility.

1. Your budget must be comprehensively and painstakingly prepared and then presented clearly and objectively to your husband and his lawyer.

2. The discussions with your husband and his lawyer must not be undertaken with an attitude of desperation or of ultimatum. The rewards of successful negotiated divorce go to those who are patient and tenacious. If you appear over-eager or if you appear as if you cannot stand another minute of contact with your

husband, even if it's just talk, then you are apt to find that your husband or his lawyer will tell your side to "take it or leave it," making continuation of bargaining difficult or even impossible.

3. Finally, harping on one monthly alimony figure or one piece of furniture or one plan of visitation usually doesn't pay. If your husband wants the sofa for sentimental reasons, he is likely to trade for it with extra alimony. If he wants to visit the children for one day at a time, rather than every other weekend for two days at a time, he is likely to bargain for that right with extra child support, or a clothing allowance (or, if not with money, then in some other way).

The marriage is over. The funeral preparations are in progress. Let the body rest in peace. Don't drag up old issues. It is because of them that there is a divorce in progress. Concentrate realistically on the new issues which you are likely to face in the future.

This does not mean that, in every dispute during the negotiations, you must be the one to give in. Quite the contrary. With children to support and (often) the best years of your life invested in the dying marriage, you must protect the interests of your children and the investment of years of your life. But today's divorce process is quiet, non-accusatory, pragmatic and negotiated. And the selection of the negotiating issues that best match the process can make a difference.

[6]

THE NEGOTIATING HUSBAND: FREEDOM THROUGH FRINGE BENEFITS

A biblical Abraham divorced his wife by simply ordering her from the house. And to this day, many a wistful—and unrealistic—male thinks he can still divorce like an Abraham.

The Romans made matters more confusing for husbands of today. They introduced alimony and then patterned getting a divorce after their most infamous invention—the Roman circus. (Cicero and other Roman lawyers made their living from divorce trials.) No wonder, then, that today many a divorcing husband thinks he must still act like a gladiator.

It was left to the early Christians to render a husband's attitude toward the divorce process not only totally unrealistic, but impossible. To St. Paul, sex was sinful and marriage the next best thing to roasting in hell. If a first marriage was bad, a second was an abomination and illegal. Reacting to the one-sidedness of the divorce of biblical times and the circus of Roman divorce, Christianity devised a simple solution: it abolished divorce altogether. Now the husband was neither king in his house nor a warrior in the courtroom. He was just trapped. No wonder then that today many husbands still wear the sackcloth of the early Christians as they enter a lawyer's office. They hope for a divorce but really believe they are hopelessly trapped—if not to a dead marriage then surely to lifelong servitude.

But times have changed. Today, the divorcing husband can move out of marriage relatively freely. He can divorce—*but with strings attached.*

Let us see how a husband can divorce and still feel free in his harness. (The following applies to those who act with or without a lawyer.)

How Is Your Wife Taking to Divorce?

The first thing you must do when you have decided that separation and divorce is for you is to pay close attention to your wife. How is she taking the idea of divorce? How does she see herself after divorce? How does she see herself going through the process of divorce? Does she talk of being reasonable? Does she express concern lest your future career be adversely affected by a messy divorce? Or does she talk of divorce with a fiery eye and a vindictive tongue?

Don't assume that your wife will behave in divorce the same way as she did in marriage. How your wife conducts herself during the divorce process may or may not be related to the way she conducted herself either when you had a good marriage or when you were thinking of breaking up. Many a woman who was meek and compliant during marriage sees the process of divorce as a way to get back at her husband—and indirectly at herself—for "the way he has treated her." She may seek a tough-minded courtroom lawyer to take up her cause. She may cease all communication with her husband and inform him that "my lawyer tells me to have nothing to do with you." But the lawyer may only be a front for her bad behavior.

On the other hand, many a wife who was strong-willed and independent during the marriage may appear reasonable and conciliatory during divorce. Her independent and self-reliant attitude, which may have wrought havoc during the marriage, may be ready-made for the process of divorce.

You should be prepared to protect yourself from the attacks of a vindictive wife or to capitalize on the advantages of negotiating with a wife who is glorying in her new opportunity for independence.

If your wife is talking reasonably and with the language of woman's independence, then perhaps you should try to stimulate preliminary negotiations with her even before either of you obtain an attorney. On the other hand, if she is brimming with anger, threatening to "take every last cent" you have, you should simply refer her to your lawyer because he is apt to have more success in cooling her down than you have had.

Your Wife's Sense of Security Can Mean Your Early Freedom

The whole tone of the negotiations is apt to be affected by what you say in the early stages of the divorce process. If you threaten not to support her and the children or if you talk of taking all the furniture, you will place her on the defensive, forcing her to greet every aspect of the negotiations with suspicion and stubbornness. If you warn her that any deal you make will have to be changed if she obtains employment, you will undoubtedly discourage her from working, thereby destroying one of the greatest financial assets of a divorced husband, his working ex-wife.

The last thing a husband wants when negotiating a divorce is a wife grasping for every penny she can get, fearful of cutting the ties that bind her, and reluctant to help herself.

You should make it clear to your wife from the very beginning that she need not be afraid, and that you will meet your obligations. You should take every advantage flowing to husbands from twentieth-century attitudes toward women's economic independence rather than sidetrack them with dubious arguments which attempt to minimize the increased responsibilities your wife will soon face.

If you are careful, you can direct the divorce negotiations away from impossible issues of "who caused the marriage to fail" and "who has the general obligation to care for a divorced wife and small children" to the realistic goal of *setting limits* on your obligations.

On the other hand, if you are not careful, you can direct your divorce down the road to a courtroom battle in which you will end up paying the bill for *both* sides.

The importance of fostering an atmosphere of responsible bargaining cannot be overemphasized: much of the bitterness of many divorces has actually been created by early exchanges of the wrong kind of attitudes.

A word of warning is in order here: do not interpret my

suggestions that you take a reasonable and perhaps even generous stance in your opening negotiations as meaning you should be overgenerous—generous beyond your financial means.

I know of a young couple who were separated and trying to negotiate a separation and property settlement agreement. The husband, an insurance salesman, had "gone through" two lawyers and started on his third. He was frustrated. He and his wife had been unable to reach an agreement. His original offers of alimony and support, property and insurance were very generous, indeed more generous than his wife needed, or, for that matter, than he could possibly afford. Because they were so generous, his wife, it seemed to his third lawyer, must have concluded that he had extra sources of income which he hadn't told her about. His flamboyant dress and bon vivant personality only served to reinforce her suspicions: she wanted even more. He offered still more, and for over a year they were caught in a circle in which his increased offers served only to increase her rising expectations.

The third lawyer, however, sat down with the husband and prepared a list of his expenses and his income. He obtained a balance sheet of the husband's assets and liabilities certified by an accountant. Before offering a new proposal for settlement of the case containing reduced amounts for alimony and support, the lawyer advised the husband to write his wife and explain that he could no longer continue to support her and the children as he had been doing without going bankrupt. (As a matter of fact, he had been steadily withdrawing from his moderate-sized savings account and had even obtained advances against future salary from his company to meet his unrealistic budget.) The husband was reluctant to take this advice. He feared an explosion.

The lawyer explained that he would have to cut down sooner

or later and psychologically his wife should be the first to hear the bad news—and from his own lips. Finally, he agreed. He announced to his wife his plan to reduce monthly payments from the interim level they had reached during their feud. He specified exactly which expenses he thought she should eliminate: an expensive lawn care service, an annual television maintenance contract and other non-essential items. She fumed, he said, about the reduction and told him he would hear from her lawyer. Within days, she sued him. In time her lawyer and his lawyer met to settle the case. Her lawyer acknowledged that both spouses had been living beyond their means and that the husband's generosity had been making the case impossible to settle. He knew that, generosity or not, a judge would never order the husband to pay the high amounts he'd once paid.

Eventually the case was settled. The negotiating "trick" that helped make it possible for the wife to agree to accept less was to give her an "escalation clause." The point here is, however, that regardless of the tricks and the subtle tax-saving devices available, the key to avoiding much of the negotiating trouble is for you, the husband, to take the lead in being as financially realistic as possible—from the very beginning. And that means not being either overgenerous or over-tight-fisted.

Stress the Importance of "Fringe Benefits"

You have a secret weapon for settling your divorce case: "fringe benefits." Perhaps the most difficult area of negotiating a separation agreement is arriving at how much alimony and child support should be paid. "Fringe benefits" can take the sharp edges off the dispute.

If your wife is like most, she is desperately afraid of the financial unknown after divorce. In particular, she probably fears her inability to meet extraordinary medical and hospital bills or other financial catastrophes. She is also worried about how the children's college education will be paid for. As a result, many a wife initially demands much more alimony and support than she needs to satisfy minimum monthly needs.

Start the negotiations by offering four specific "fringe benefits" to your wife *before* you tangle with the question of how much alimony and support you should pay. They are:

1. Medical and hospital insurance.
2. Life insurance.
3. Enough of an interest in your house—or the equivalent cash—so your wife can remain in it or buy a new house for her and the children.
4. Provision for the children's college education.

How much of each you offer depends on your means, the family needs and how badly each of you wants a divorce.

1. *Medical and hospital insurance.* If your wife knows from the outset of the negotiations that her children's major medical and hospital expenses will be automatically paid by an insurance company, which is, by its nature, a responsible and impartial provider, she will be less inclined to worry about extra alimony and support to cover these items. The probable result to you will be smaller monthly alimony and support payments.

2. *Life insurance.* In the same way, if your wife knows from the outset of the negotiations that if and when you die, she will receive a substantial amount of cash from an insurance company (to take the place of the support payments which terminate on your death), she will be less inclined to hold out for extra cash, or a larger portion of the family savings or securities, or a higher alimony and support payment, in order to protect herself against

the money problems she would have if you died. Again, the probable result to you will be a more advantageous property settlement in most every aspect.

3. *A house.* If you permit your wife to live in your present house or if you encourage her with financial aid to move into a house titled in her name, your divorcing wife obtains additional financial and emotional security to fall back on. She is therefore less likely to seek monthly alimony and support payments that you would regard as excessive.

4. *Provide for the children's college education.* If your wife knows from the beginning of negotiations that your children will receive a college education because there is a fund set aside for that purpose (which she can add to), she will be less inclined to feel she is endangering her children's right to a college education by divorcing their father. The result to you is apt to be a quieter and quicker settlement.

You probably provided each of these fringe benefits long before you thought of divorce. They have long been a part of your "family overhead." Therefore, it is not too difficult a step for you to continue to pay the insurance premiums and provide for college. The alternative, to institute a new schedule of higher alimony and support payments designed to cover the same items, is clearly a less attractive option.

With each "fringe benefit" you counter effectively your wife's compelling argument that she is being left all alone with the obligations of raising the children and maintaining a home for them, except for the alimony and support she receives from you. She will feel freer to negotiate about alimony, support, custody and the divorce itself with a greater reserve and a greater sense of security.

The whole negotiating process will take on a less desperate

climate when your wife learns that the family concern will continue as usual: same or similar house, same expectations about the children's health care and education. (Only the husband will be gone, which you must admit is probably what she wants, now that you have both decided to divorce.)

Try to Set the Rules of the Alimony Negotiations

1. *Deduct the insurance premium from your negotiating budget.* As you smooth your trip toward divorce by providing the fringe benefits outlined above, don't forget to include their cost when you prepare your negotiating budget.

For example, if you earn $15,000 a year after taxes and your wife has her sights set on obtaining 50 percent of your income after taxes to support herself and your three children, you should not forget to reduce the amount of your income that will be available for alimony and support by what you will be paying for the fringe benefits. So, from the $15,000 you should deduct the $1000 a year you pay in life and medical and hospital insurance premiums, and the $500 a year you propose to continue to contribute to the children's college education fund.

2. *Deduct the higher income taxes from your negotiating budget.* Be sure to subtract not merely the amount of the income taxes you paid when you and your wife lived together; also subtract the extra income taxes you must pay when you lose the right to file a joint income tax return and the lower rate that goes with it. Recompute your taxes as a single taxpayer, before you commence negotiations.

3. *Deduct retirement and pension allowances from your negotiating budget.* Money withheld by your employer for retirement

(or by yourself if you are a self-employed person in a Keogh Plan) will not be available to spend for years to come. So, you should not agree to pay current alimony and support based on money you do not actually have. Your wife and children will eventually receive the benefit of the money that is being withheld for your retirement: when you retire, you will be paying her alimony from your retirement pension check. So, she, in fairness, should budget her future in the same way that you do.

Consider this example:

Assume you earn $15,000 a year.

Before the divorce you paid about $2250 in income taxes. After you are divorced, you will pay about $2650 in income taxes since you can no longer file a joint income tax return. Subtract $2650 (not $2250) from your negotiating budget.

Your employer withholds $100 a month from your salary as your contribution to the company retirement plan. Subtract $1200 from your negotiating budget.

You also pay $350 a year in premiums for $20,000 of life insurance, $200 a year in premiums for disability insurance, $300 a year in premiums for hospital and medical insurance and contribute $500 a year toward a college education fund. Subtract $1350 from your negotiating budget.

Thus, you should reduce the income available to pay alimony and support by $5200. Your net income available to negotiate for alimony and support will shrink to $9800. Therefore, when you agree to pay your wife 50 percent of your net income, you will be agreeing to pay her $4900 a year.

If you fail to recompute your taxes based on the single taxpayer rates, and if you fail to reduce your income available for alimony and support by the cost of the other "fringe benefits," your net income available to negotiate alimony and support will be $12,750 and your alimony and support payment will be $6375.

Thus, a careful analysis by you of your budget and the expense of providing valuable "fringe benefits" can save you, in this case, $1475 a year, the difference between $4900 and $6375.

When you add to this saving the additional saving which comes from deducting some of the payment as alimony on your tax return, the total can be considerable. For example, if $2400 of the $4900 annual alimony and support payment is allocated to alimony in the agreement, you, as a single rate taxpayer, will be able to save about $440 in taxes.

Thus, instead of paying $6375 a year (by allocating all payments as child support, by not recomputing taxes at the individual rate and failing to deduct retirement plan and college education contributions and insurance premiums) you will pay about $4460 each year ($4900 less the $440 alimony deduction tax refund).

The result: about $1915 of savings each year ($4460 per year rather than $6375 per year).

This can mean the difference between just making it month to month and being able to live comfortably.

Bargain for the Chance to Be a Father Instead of a "Check-Writing Machine"

The best time to negotiate over your future relationship with your children is when you announce you will provide "fringe benefits" to your wife and children. You should ask her to give you the right to deduct from the amount you must pay her for alimony and support a small amount which you can "voluntarily" use for the children in your own way.

After the divorce, many a father comes to feel that he is nothing to his children but a check-writing machine. Moreover, he often cannot afford to be more than a check-writer even if he wants to, because his monthly obligations to his divorced family use up every dollar he has, thereby embittering him in the process.

The relationship between a divorced father and his children is perpetually in danger of deteriorating into empty ritual. So, a father who is able to take his children for a vacation trip or who is able to suggest and pay for piano lessons or an Easter outfit at least has a fighting chance to perpetuate what might have been —or begin what never was.

Trying Harder for No. 2

Many a husband argues to his wife that he cannot afford to pay all the alimony and support she wants—or even needs—because he must have enough left over to support a new wife and a new family if and when he remarries. As his wife's blood pressure begins to rise, he quickly adds that he has no present plans to remarry and she should "cool down" because he has not been "fooling around." By then the damage has been done—often irreversibly—because, from then on, every time he complains in the negotiations about his inability to meet his wife's demands for alimony and support, she will counter with the argument that his present family comes first or that he must "meet first obligations first," or that he should have thought about providing for the possibly overwhelming demands of two families before he decided to separate, etc., etc.

You can avoid all this by *verbally* ignoring the subject of your remarriage. Both you and your wife know that the chances are that each of you will remarry. Although, as a general rule, neither has a special person in mind at the time of the divorce, each of you should know that eight out of ten divorced spouses remarry.

Remarrying is a fact of life. But not all the facts of life should be shouted out loud. The lawyer's office is not the place for discussion of your remarriage. You will gain nothing by reminding your wife (who is about to embark upon a new and uncertain world—the world of a divorced woman with children) that her source of financial security may also be your second wife's. While she may logically realize that remarriage is inevitable, it may be far more difficult for her to accept that fact emotionally.

This does not mean that you should ignore the likelihood of your remarriage when you negotiate your divorce. There is a way for you to protect your remarried future. When you prepare your budget to present to your wife or her lawyer, be sure to estimate generously your expenses for rent, food, clothing and other expenses for yourself so that they are on the high side of what would be normal for you: a slightly more expensive apartment, eating out more often than usual, etc. While this approach will not necessarily cover all the expenses of the maintenance of the second family, it will make a substantial dent in them. To this "dent" can be added the extra tax relief you will receive from being able once again to file a married taxpayer's joint return at an advantageous tax rate as well as sharing in any income your new wife may earn.

You should resign yourself to indirect methods of budgeting the costs of a new family—rather than heavy-handedly interjecting them directly.

Consider the Lump Sum

You may have read about a wife receiving a large sum of money in a property settlement agreement instead of receiving alimony. Your wife may have read this too. For the wife, the lump sum seems to satisfy some kind of a demand for payment for "services rendered," or for "losing the best years" of her life, or to satisfy a desire for revenge or a need to have something to brag about to her friends or family.

For the husband there are both advantages and disadvantages aying his wife a lump sum instead of monthly alimony.

ne advantages are simplicity and emotional freedom. Since lump sum payment is customarily paid by the husband to the *instead* of alimony, it terminates once and for all your ncial obligations to your wife. And the one-time payment inates the need for any contact with your wife once you the payment.

e principal disadvantage is that under present law you forthe alimony deduction on your income tax return (unless you it in installments that are spread over more than ten years, unless the payments are made to terminate on the wife's death remarriage).

Also, the lump sum payment is not a realistic method of eliminating future contact in the event that you have children whom you must still support. Since you must continue to have contact with your wife—at least to the extent of sending her monthly child support checks—the value in the one-shot lump sum payment, in minimizing contact with your wife, all but disappears.

An ex-wife may forget about the lump sum payment she received at the time of divorce when years later she complains about the inadequacy of the child support payments and seeks an increase. So, when you have children to support, reject a lump sum approach and pay the alimony along with the child support (taking the deduction on your income tax return for the alimony payment). You will enlarge the amount of that monthly check you send to your wife and thereby minimize her case years later when she claims your total monthly contributions are too low.

Don't Covet Your Wife's Earnings, Praise Them

Many a husband brings to the negotiating table one particular attitude regarding his wife's income which often returns to haunt him. He announces that he has heard that since he and his wife have separated his wife has found a job or is training herself for a profession. He then demands a reduction in the size of his alimony and support payments.

This heavy-handed reaction to the news that his wife is working (or may soon have income of her own) ignores the fact that a wife with extra income naturally will be inclined at the time of divorce to be less demanding.

Your announcement that you intend to lay claim to her earnings is apt to elicit an equal and opposite reaction of stubbornness on her part, particularly when it comes to her justifying high amounts in her budget for clothing, entertainment, automobile expenses and other non-food-and-rent items. Or, you may find that your wife will change her plans and refuse to work, just to spite you. Because she may not have worked since the early years of her marriage, her failure to work may not be held against her by the judge. (In fact, for fear of jeopardizing their alimony and support payments, many wives refuse to go to work for years after their divorce.)

Your wife's future income from her own employment can

make a difference, not only to her, but to you. It can avoid years of just "getting by," and years of continual friction caused by demands by your ex-wife for more alimony and child support. Husbands often forget that it is the woman's greater financial independence that has made today's easy divorce possible. If you recognize that every cent your wife earns on her own will benefit you indirectly (as well as your children directly), you will master an important truth about today's negotiating process. As the years go by and your wife needs additional money, she may not think of that ex-husband who grasped for a share of her earnings. Rather, she may remember that you specifically made no claim to her earnings with the understanding that she would try to meet any new needs on her own without bothering you for an increase in alimony and support. And there is yet another reason for you to encourage your wife to work. Somewhere in the professional and business world she will enter, there may well be a new husband waiting for her. And, with her new husband comes your freedom from alimony.

Pro's and Con's of the Escalation Clause

There may come a time in the negotiations when both you and your wife will realize that she honestly needs more alimony and support than you can afford to pay. There is a way to bridge this seemingly impossible chasm: The Escalation Clause. This is a clause in the separation agreement that provides that you will automatically pay a portion of your additional income to your wife as extra alimony and child support, if and when your income goes up.

Sometimes, the only alternative to an escalation clause is a lawsuit by your wife which seeks more support and alimony than you can possibly pay. This will cause both her and you anguish, attorney's fees and ill will, and will usually benefit no one. The judge will not be any more successful in increasing your income than you will be in reducing the needs of your wife and children. The judge may try to strike a middle ground with a compromise amount, but that too will make neither you nor your wife happy. Moreover, going to court will not establish the machinery for automatic increases based on your increased income because judges do not deal in escalation clauses.

This does not mean that, in every case, the husband should volunteer to escalate. The escalation clause can result in making you pay more than your wife actually needs.* It can also result in making you pay more of an increase than she'd ever seek in the future. Many women shun the thought of going to court. In addition to the humiliation of asking a stranger to settle personal family problems and the added cost of an attorney's fee, many wives hesitate to make a plea to a judge for increased support and alimony for fear the judge will—instead of increasing—*reduce* the existing schedule of support and alimony payments, or for fear the ex-husband will demand more visits to his children as a compensation for the increased payments. Thus, you should propose an escalation clause either as a last resort—to break a stalemate in the negotiations—or if you wish to be extra-generous—voluntarily.

"Don't Make a Move . . . ."

The major concept for the husband to keep in mind is that, in most families, he has the money. It is the wife who is the moving

* If it is strictly geared to your increased income and not to your wife's increased needs, you could guard against this by imposing a maximum or a sliding scale of payments.

force, the "have not," as it were, in the monetary negotiations. She must make the demands for money and, in the end, it is the husband who bears the brunt in deciding whether and how well to meet them.

Just because your wife makes threats or gives you an ultimatum does not mean that you must do likewise. You can usually afford to sit back and endure them, and later purchase a great many concessions with your own "concession" to pay reasonable alimony and support. You can bargain for better visitation arrangements, for your wife's agreement to pay her own attorney's fees, or for the right to receive a larger share of the proceeds from the sale of the house.

Or, you can make certain in the agreement that you will be the one to take the children as dependents on your income tax return rather than your wife, thereby insuring that you will get the $650* per child exemption on your tax return.

These benefits—while not all financial—are very real ones. During life after divorce, they can become more and more important. The most common divorce today, according to the Bureau of Vital Statistics of the United States Department of Health, Education and Welfare is that of a couple in their thirties with one or two young children. Thus for ten or fifteen years, most husbands will be absentee fathers. Before you bargain away your rights with respect to the children and their mother, you should ponder what provisions can make those next ten or fifteen years—and the payments each month during those years—more meaningful. Then you should be certain those provisions are in the agreement. They might include a voice in choosing the colleges in which the children are enrolled, what church they attend, what city they live in and its proximity to your own home and many more considerations, often limited to

* $700 in 1972; $750 in 1973 and thereafter.

the circumstances of your family.

Earlier in this book I tried to dispel the notion that paying alimony is always bad: there are circumstances when paying alimony can actually save you money. Likewise, there are circumstances when *staying power* can also save you money. If your wife is more eager for the divorce—or for you to vacate the house or apartment—you may find the last—and perhaps only—time in your marriage when the very things that are compelling your wife to end the marriage can "pay off." For you may actually enhance your bargaining position by refusing to move out until you have negotiated an agreement that meets with your satisfaction.

Of course, if you are the one who cannot stand life at home a moment longer, this advice may not be realistic. If you can hold out, many a separation agreement has been drafted much closer to a husband's liking because he chose to sit it out, and not, like Dagwood Bumstead, indignantly stalk out.

[7]

HOW TO USE A LAWYER

Generally, lawyers charge for three things: their time, the difficulties they encounter, and the results they obtain.

If your case takes a long time to negotiate, and if the negotiations are interrupted by courthouse interludes, time-consuming depositions, or lengthy bargaining sessions not only between the lawyers, but between you and your lawyer, your bill will be higher. On the other hand, if you and your spouse do your homework, bring to the bargaining table a clear idea of your needs and the ability of each to meet them, and an attitude of flexibility and compromise, then the time it takes to negotiate your divorce can be relatively short and the price lower. (This is a "sweetener" which you ought to consider as a possible incentive to compromise.)

When Your Lawyer Asks for a Retainer . . .

Most lawyers charge a retainer—or down payment—when they first take your case. The amount of the retainer depends on what you and your lawyer estimate is at stake, how reasonable you and your spouse are likely to be, and what difficulties the lawyer can expect to face. Still another factor is the wealth and size of the community in which the lawyer practices. When all these factors are taken together, the result can swing widely—anywhere from $200 to $2500—with each of the factors affecting not only the amount of the retainer but the final fee in the case.

Many a wife finds herself without personal funds just at the very time when she needs a lawyer. If you are in such a position you have three alternatives: (1) You can approach a lawyer on the basis of an agreement that in the end your husband will pay, or can be made to pay, the lawyer's bill. (Some attorneys will flatly refuse such an arrangement.) (2) You can borrow the amount of the retainer and hope your husband will reimburse you as part of the over-all settlement. (3) You can insist that your husband pay your lawyer's bill at the *beginning* of the case.

I emphatically recommend the last alternative, and, failing that course, the second. It is better, not just for the lawyer, but for you and your husband too, that he be paid his retainer at the beginning.

You may feel that as a lawyer I am only looking out for lawyers' interests in offering this advice. But think it over. A lawyer who has not been paid a reasonable retainer in the beginning of a divorce case and who may feel uncertain that he will ever be paid is not in the best position to negotiate for the wife. He is apt to weaken too soon and counsel you to "get it over with." After all, he is only human—although technically he is supposed to be above such petty motives.

As far as husbands are concerned, they are likely to have to pay less to their wives' lawyers if they have not forced them to wait until the end of the negotiations. As the negotiations drag on, everyone realizes the value of winding matters up and becomes eager for the divorce. It is then that the lawyers with the worst reputations for charging too much in the divorce cases try to blow up the whole deal unless they are paid an exorbitant fee.

So, the most realistic approach to lawyers' fees is to (1) coolly appraise what kind of a case you have; (2) get a lawyer who can negotiate (without dragging you through the courts or selling you out in an armchair giveaway) and (3) pay him enough in advance to insure he is on your side *only*, with the same thing at stake as you have—getting you the best deal as quickly and quietly as possible.

Getting Started

Assuming you have found the right lawyer, you will need to explain your circumstances, your needs and goals. One good method is to try to write the story of your marriage. You will discover that thinking and writing about what went wrong with your marriage is far more constructive than thinking about how to accuse your husband of cruelty or your wife of adultery. You will realize that many of your problems have grown out of causes which arose long before the marriage went sour.

As you put "the problem" on paper, you will arrive at a kind of new objectivity that you probably have not yet been able to muster. Emotion, hate, disgust, fear will gradually give way to reason—cooler, quieter and more manageable.

You may not find answers to your problems. You may not find justification for your spouse's misconduct. But you will find understanding and an ability to communicate that understanding better to yourself and to others.

From your lawyer's point of view, by writing about yourself and your marriage, you will be a better client because you will have learned to think more objectively and less emotionally and can thus keep the other side's point of view in mind.

Once having written down the story of your divorce, your lawyer will, on the basis of what he has read, open a series of private and confidential talks with you about your needs and plans. At the heart of these discussions is the question of money. That is why it is essential to prepare a "separation budget."

The Separation Budget

Begin by thinking about what life will be like when your spouse is not around. Make a list of the expenses you (and, if you are to have custody, the children) will have when you are living separately. Your lawyer will find this document invaluable when he meets with your spouse's lawyer.

In a typical situation, a wife with custody of the children might prepare the following budget:

Divorced Wife's Budget—Including Children

Rent (apartment or house, including real estate taxes)
Utilities

- Gas
- Oil
- Electricity
- Water and Garbage Collection
- Telephone

Food Costs
- At Home
- Lunches for the children at school
- Lunches for you (if you decide to work)

Insurance (hospital, medical, house, car, etc.)
- For yourself
- For the children

Cosmetics and Beauty Parlor

Entertainment
- For You
- For the Children

School fees, supplies and allowances

Automobile
- Maintenance
- Gas
- Tags
- Replacement

Vacations

Savings

Taxes (Federal, State and Local Income Taxes)
- On your income
- On alimony

A *husband's budget* may cover many of the same basic items but would have to provide, of course, for alimony, child support, and the costs of maid service and laundry. He might want to add a little extra for savings (against the day when he remarries) and include provision for extra expenses when the children come for a protracted visit.

Learning to Negotiate

When a wife goes over her budget with her lawyer, the chances are that she will realize that her husband will not be able to pay her all that she and the children need if they wish to maintain their pre-divorce standard of living.

Sometimes, if there are many children or special needs, such as an ill wife or child, a husband can be made to pay more, but ordinarily, between 50 and 60 percent of his after-tax income is the limit a husband must pay to his ex-wife and children and 30 or 40 percent is common.

But, if you both learn to negotiate and to *think flexibly,* you will find that there are practical solutions to your problems. For example, if the husband wants more visits with the children, the wife might bargain for the title to the house or his promise to pay for the children's college education. By bargaining, each of you will eventually end up with much of what you want and need.

Instead of dwelling on the past mistakes and wrongs of the marriage, plan on *not* making new ones. Taking a giant step toward answering the particular needs of your new household and standard of living, demonstrate to your lawyer that you are approaching your divorce in a calm and careful way. By setting the negotiating atmosphere in your relations with your own lawyer, with your spouse and with your spouse's lawyer, you will be going a long way toward ensuring that your divorce will be negotiated and not litigated.

The Grim Alternative

Of course, there is another approach to divorce: litigation through a courtroom trial with a courtroom lawyer. But it is far more likely that by taking this route each of you will get less than you could have gotten by negotiation.

Let us see what happens in a typical non-negotiated divorce.

The big troubles usually start when one or both of the spouses select a lawyer who does not recognize that divorce by negotiation is preferable to divorce by court battles. A lawyer writes a threatening "lawyer letter." Your lawyer replies with a similarly charged letter. Then the lawyers go through the motions of a perfunctory settlement conference at which no one really tries to settle the problems amicably. Instead, each makes impossible demands and throws up his hands in desperation at his opponent's unreasonableness.

Then, one spouse may surprise the other by filing suit for divorce or for alimony and child support—on inflammatory grounds. The person who is sued experiences the embarrassment, frustration and indignation of having a sheriff deposit papers on an office desk or at the front door.

In those lawsuit papers the person who first sues calls the other person all sorts of names. The names can really hurt this time because they are in writing, in a place for all the world to see (if all the world cares to), and in the moralistic and obsolete prose of the "divorce lawyer."

"Your complainant," the lawsuit might begin, "respectfully represents to this honorable court . . . that on or about the 11th day of September, 1969, the defendant did, without just cause, enter into a cruel course of conduct, to wit, she refused to have sexual relations with your complainant, and, as a result of the cruelty as aforesaid, your complainant was compelled to leave the marital bedroom in order to preserve his self-respect . . . . "

Your wife reads all the charges in the lawsuit served on her —and calls her lawyer immediately: "I've been sued. I told you we should have sued first. When can I see you?" She then responds to attack by answering with a general denial of all the charges and a list of some counter-charges of her own.

"Your counter-claimant," a typical counter-suit would wail, "respectfully represents to this honorable court that for over two years, the plaintiff, did without just cause refuse to have sexual relations with your counter-claimant. Your counter-claimant discovered evidence indicating that on or about [various dates], the plaintiff committed adultery with Jane Doe of Pittsburgh, Pennsylvania; that thereafter the plaintiff, when confronted with the evidence, admitted such acts of adultery; that, as a result, your counter-claimant removed herself from the bedroom of the parties and has not, since her discovery of said adultery condoned same."

And so war escalates. If this had happened with the Joneses, whose case I discussed in chapter 1, the course of their divorce could go something like this:

Mrs. Jones' non-negotiating lawyer would realize that her husband's admission of adultery and the motel receipts still might not be enough evidence by themselves to prove the adultery. Her lawyer might need proof of Mr. Jones' "adulterous disposition," as well as his "adulterous opportunity." So this lawyer would recommend that a detective interview the manager of the Pittsburgh motel who had, when Mrs. Jones called him, admitted that he saw Mr. Jones and a woman holding hands and kissing outside the motel about 1:00 A.M. But since the motel clerk carefully reminds the detective that he was on duty for only a half hour after he saw the husband go into the motel room and the lights were never turned out during that time, the detective must find and interview the relief clerk too.

After the motel clerks are interviewed, Mrs. Jones' lawyer would probably decide to preserve their testimony, officially, in case the clerks later became unavailable as witnesses. He directs the sheriff to deliver papers to the two motel clerks commanding them, by order of the judge of the divorce court, to come to his office and testify in the case of Jones versus Jones. He sends a copy of the paper to Mr. Jones' lawyer, who attends to hear the testimony. The court reporter takes down the questions and answers in shorthand and transcribes his notes into a booklet (called a deposition transcript) at approximately $1.10 per page. So far, aside from lawyer's fees, all this would easily cost Mr. Jones $750.

After the depositions, Mr. Jones' lawyer reports the details to Mr. Jones. Mr. Jones explodes: "Who's going to pay for all this?"

"The way this is going, you will," his lawyer must truthfully respond.

"The reporter's time, the detective's trip, the witness fees and the transcript of the depositions and the two lawyers' fees?" Mr. Jones will cry.

"I'm afraid so," his non-negotiating lawyer will answer.

"Well, if I'm going to have to pay for all this, I'm going to make her sorry she ever started this. I'm going to tell the judge about all the nutty things she does in bed and how she finally had to go to a psychiatrist. In fact, let's take her psychiatrist's deposition."

"We can't do that," his lawyer would have to say. "The judge won't make him testify because there is a confidential relationship between a doctor and a patient and anything a patient tells her doctor is wrapped in secrecy."

"Well, she told her mother and a friend of ours all the bizzare things she does in bed. I don't know why she told them, but she did. Let's take *their* depositions. And what about hitting her where it hurts? Can't we claim she's not a fit mother? I heard that some guy wrote that he'd wished he'd done that when he was in a divorce case."

"Even if your wife were an unfit mother, how could you take care of two little girls, aged four and six, when you're traveling on the road half the time and downtown at work the other half?" the lawyer wonders.

"Listen, Mr. Lawyer. Who's running this case anyway? I think you're letting her lawyer walk all over you."

And so the non-negotiating lawyer floats along with his client—sometimes leading him, sometimes being led—down the road of litigated divorce. The costs mount and time passes. Mr. and Mrs. Jones gradually destroy whatever ability they once had to maintain a decent relationship after divorce.

The trial undoubtedly brings more of the same. The new element is the judge. Typically, he enters the courtroom for yet another day of his three-month term in matrimonial court.

The judge knows very well that the charges and countercharges do not tell the real story of the Joneses' family problems. He knows that there is a whole world of unhappiness—caused by emotional tension, financial strain, lack of understanding, tired nights after tiring sales trips and pressured days of taking kids to and from their lessons. He knows that gradually this couple's ability to understand—if indeed there ever had been real understanding—has been eroded.

While the lawyers bicker about some technical point, the judge is apt to be computing how much money Mr. Jones should pay Mrs. Jones and the children. He totals Mr. Jones' list of expenses for maintaining himself alone. Then he subtracts $50 (just because the judge knows everybody pads a little anyway). That leaves $450 a month available for Mrs. Jones and the children.

Then the judge looks at Mrs. Jones' budget. He knows at a glance that she and the children need $550 a month to continue to live at the same standard they had been accustomed to. But he also knows that is impossible now, that no man can really maintain two households as well as he once maintained one.

"She will be able to work in a few years," the judge is likely to reason to himself, "and I've got to order Mr. Jones to pay her lawyer a fee. He will need to borrow to pay that fee and that of his own lawyer too. I'll order $400 a month alimony and support," he silently concludes at the end of the testimony, and the lawyers can divide it up any way they want. He announces that the court will take a ten-minute recess and tells the lawyers what he is thinking. Hastily, the lawyers arbitrarily allocate $100 of the $400 to alimony and $300 to child support. Of course, there is no chance to bargain about tax consequences of the allocation.

Then, the judge returns and orders that each party is to receive half of the equity in the house after it is sold.

So, the husband is saddled with alimony and cannot minimize or maximize the tax advantages or the disadvantages of it.

So, the wife must move from the house.

So, the husband must pay higher bills and court costs.

The question is: was it worth it?

What about the adultery, the wife's bedroom behavior, and the rest? The judge will listen to all of it but is likely to conclude: "they cancel each other out." He will announce that "the court will 'award' Mrs. Jones a divorce on the ground of cruelty." "The marriage was dead anyway," the judge will think as he leaves the courtroom, "or at least it was dying by the time that husband and wife started the process of getting a divorce. From then on it was just torture for everyone."

Judges can rarely make ideal compromises if they have to work them out by themselves from the bench while listening with half-an-ear to what most of them have come to regard as a useless and irrelevant wrangle. Points are left out. Mistakes are made. Costs mount.

That is why most judges are extremely pleased when counsel for the opposing parties can settle these questions through negotiated agreement.

Fortunately, most of the time, this is what happens. The courtroom trial occurs only in a minority of divorce cases. The spotlight has largely shifted from the courtroom to the lawyer's office—and anyone who studies the matter coolly can see why.

[8]

DIVORCE: FROM THE BIBLE TO THE PILL

"Divorce is a drastic piece of surgery, the unnatural severing of what should be one and indivisible. As such it is bound to cause pain and loss and leave lasting scars. To demand that a divorce law shall let no one be hurt is therefore to ask the impossible."*

But unhappy spouses need not suffer until the laws of divorce become perfect. By negotiating their divorce, they have within their control the power to keep their divorce private and decent. They can bypass those written laws of divorce that are still a

* "A Divorce Law for Contemporary Society," a report wryly entitled "Putting Asunder," written in 1966 by a group of scholars appointed by the Archbishop of Canterbury.

patchwork of cruelty, confusion and condescension and obtain their divorce with dignity.

Our Divorce Heritage: Freedom of Choice—and the Double Standard

America's melting pot of legal attitudes has not made the job of divorcing with dignity an easy one.

The Hebrews gave us dreams of a free choice of a mate, but they also firmly grafted the Double Standard onto our divorce laws.

The Romans perfected divorce by mutual consent but also gave us careful lessons on how to turn the divorce court into a circus.

The early Christians preached to us to be more kind to divorcing mothers but then suggested there could be a profit in divorce, just before they abolished divorce altogether.

The Reformation gave us back divorce but forgot to eliminate the requirement that there be grounds.

The New World gave us room to run away from one marriage and the frame of mind to conceive of a second one as better, but, in the Reno divorce, created a new pervasive disrespect for divorce altogether.

As a result, our attitudes toward divorce are as confused and contradictory as the laws are.

Our Family Heritage: Fragile and Fast-changing

Changes in the very institution of the family have also taken their toll on the process of divorce. People have increasingly come to look upon marriage not merely for the stabilizing purpose of rearing children and inheriting property but for more tenuous ends like personality fulfillment, emotional strength to fight against the pressures of an urban life, and the most intimate companionship a couple will ever know in their lives.

Gone is the large family of aunts, uncles, cousins, parents and grandparents, all living in the same town or village and providing support, companionship and an economic way of life for a husband and wife. Instead, there is geographic mobility, the American ideal of freedom of choice, the shadowy anonymity of urban life and the unfettered right to pursue happiness, individually, perhaps without the help of or responsibility to anyone.

Others Have Trouble with Divorce Too

The struggle for divorce with dignity has not been difficult only for Americans. Other nations have had difficulty with this problem of divorce too.

In Moslem countries, a husband can divorce a wife at will, but the wife cannot get a divorce. The husband need only tell her "I divorce you," three times in front of two witnesses and he is divorced. No alimony. No questions. No delay. But the rate of divorce is one out of two marriages, compared to our one in four, and Moslem women are desperately engaged in trying to change the unfairness of their system.

In Spain, Argentina and many other conservative Catholic countries, there is no divorce at all, but neither is there general satisfaction with the system or wide respect for marriage vows.

In many of the Communist Eastern European countries, the granting of a divorce is up to a government administrator: if divorces are being encouraged that year, there is no trouble; but if baby output is down and there have been too many divorces lately, the administrator may get orders from the central planners to deny them. Policies can and have changed almost annually.

The Pill and the Abortion

Yet, in America, there are some changes that bode well both for the institution of marriage and for the lot of those who must seek a divorce.

For almost ten years, despite many misconceptions, the divorce rate has not increased. What has increased is the number of children who have become involved in a divorced marriage. Today, about 600,000 children each year become children of divorce. But, here, the Pill, and other contraceptive methods now being developed—and changes in the laws governing abortion—will undoubtedly have their greatest impact.

The Pill will probably delay the marriage of many who marry for sex and then find they have created a child in a marriage they no longer want.*

Increased use of the Pill—and legalized abortion—will undoubtedly prevent more and more unwanted births. The birth rate has already shown a decided drop in the United States. In 1968, it had declined nearly 20 percent from the post-war high in 1957 even though weddings were at an all-time high. A recent study in Sweden has indicated that as a result of the Pill, the rate of births to number of intercourses has declined to one birth for every 1100 intercourses.

* Even before the Pill, the average age that men and women married had dropped to twenty-three and twenty, respectively. Now, the increasing number of young people who go to college has stabilized that trend toward younger marriages: college graduates today marry later: twenty-six for men and twenty-four for women.

Other factors also serve to minimize the adverse effects of the high rate of divorce. There are more remarriages than ever before: roughly one out of every five marriages is a *re*marriage and roughly eight out of every ten divorced men and women remarry. While the rate of failure of second marriages is high, still 60 percent succeed.

The ability of women—including divorced women—to find responsible and well-paying jobs is increasing. In fact, the history of divorce is, to a large extent, the history of women's struggle for economic, social and political independence.*

Americans may not be able to do much about reducing the high *rate* of divorce. The age-old causes of divorce still remain: they are the problems of financial management, personality conflict, sexual maladjustment, parental friction; they are the problems of women exiled in the suburbs, problems of overworked company executives spending too much time on the road. And there may even be some "new" causes for divorce: the Pill may make liberated wives too demanding in bed for tired males, or the increasing economic independence of women may mean that thousands of "trapped" wives may be more willing to risk a divorce.

But Americans are doing something about the divorce laws so that when a marriage must break, at least the laws need not add insult to injury.

The Laws Are Changing

The length of time a husband or wife must live in a state in order to be able to apply for a divorce is being shortened. The geographic mobility of the American family is now recognized by

* All over the world, divorce rates tend to increase as women gain an increasing measure of equal rights.

the written laws of divorce. Most states have already reduced the time to one year—and some to six months or even six weeks. In an age of the jet airplane, interstate highway systems and corporations who often transfer executives and their families to an office in another state, the residence requirement is no longer the effective deterrent to getting a divorce that it once was.

The grounds for divorce in many states include "living apart" as well as the traditional "fault" grounds. History has shown that the acid test of whether a marriage is still alive is whether the husband and wife can and are still living together. Every state, including New York, now provides grounds for divorce other than merely adultery. Surely, this reflects the basic desire of most Americans to insure that divorce be civilized.

And the written laws are going further. In California, the Governor's Commission on the Family proposed that divorce be granted merely upon proof of the breakdown of the marriage, and in 1969 the California legislature agreed. Fifteen other states as well as Puerto Rico already had such laws. A committee of scholars appointed by the Archbishop of Canterbury in England proposed, and in 1970 Parliament enacted, the addition of "living apart" as a ground for divorce, and Canada has recently enacted such a ground.

Lawyers and laymen on the California Governor's Commission which proposed the "no fault" approach to divorce for their state* knew that the chances are that adding such a ground for divorce could hardly increase the rate of divorce in California. In California, one out of every two marriages already ended in divorce. In some parts of the state, such as Los Angeles and San Mateo counties, the rate was already as high as six and seven out of every ten marriages.

* See p. 31.

Even in non-negotiated divorces, more and more judges are minimizing the importance of who was "at fault" for the breakdown of the marriage when they decide questions of money and custody. (This rule, of course, goes for negotiated divorce too.) Judges—as well as negotiating spouses—recognize that how much alimony and support a wife and children need, how much a husband can afford to pay, and in whose custody the children will be better off are questions that require careful and practical treatment—as far removed as possible from the often emotional and speculative considerations relating to who and what caused the marriage to fail.

Some states no longer require a husband and wife who have already negotiated their divorce and separation agreement to *sue* one another for a divorce. These states have rejected illogical deference to the idea that appearances of an adversary system —of a dispute—must be maintained, even when there is no longer any dispute. In fact, the California Governor's Commission on the Family recommended that husbands and wives *should not even be allowed* to sue each other. Today, in California, when a couple cannot settle out of court, one or both of them merely apply for a judge's help in a case entitled "in the matter of the Jones family." While both can present their side, all appearances of a husband *versus* a wife are minimized. A family is involved.

The problem is age-old: how do we balance man's—and woman's—desire to be free with their ideal of a stable family system. But until all attitudes toward divorce coalesce into an elaborate fabric of well-reasoned, uniform and efficient rules, negotiating provides the most decent and dignified route out of any unhappy marriage. "The idea of bargaining may seem prosaic when matched against some of the great ideals and utopias of human aspiration," Professor Daniel Bell of Harvard's Sociology Department has observed. But for husband and wives who must divorce, it is the method that can achieve their goal with the least damage for all concerned.

APPENDIX

Most Commonly Used Grounds for Divorce and Residence Requirements

for the fifty states, the District of Columbia, the Virgin Islands, Puerto Rico, Canada and Chihuahua, Mexico, compiled as of approximately Jan. 1, 1970

The following list of grounds for divorce and residence requirements is intended as a preliminary reference. It contains only the most commonly used grounds and not those found in some states, which are rarely used, such as impotency, conviction of a crime and bestiality. Likewise, for brevity's sake, I have classified as cruelty, or desertion, or non-support, grounds which may vary from state to state in their statutory wording or in the degree or kind of proof they require. Also, I have listed only the most generally applicable residence requirement for each jurisdiction. For the application of these laws and the exception that may or may not apply, consult the statute and a local lawyer.

ALABAMA

Grounds: Adultery

Cruelty

Desertion for one year

Habitual drunkenness or drug addiction

Two years' passage of time after decree of legal separation for cruelty or for any cause justifying divorce

Husband's non-support for two years

Residence: One year by plaintiff, with certain exceptions

ALASKA

Grounds: Adultery

Cruelty

Desertion for one year

Incompatibility of temperament

Habitual and gross drunkenness for one year

Husband's non-support for one year

Drug addiction

Residence: One year by plaintiff, with certain exceptions

ARIZONA

Grounds: Adultery

Cruelty

Desertion for one year

Habitual intemperance

Husband's non-support for one year

Living apart for five years

Residence: One year by plaintiff

GROUNDS FOR DIVORCE

ARKANSAS

Grounds: Adultery
Cruelty
Desertion for one year
Habitual drunkenness for one year
Living apart for three years
Husband's non-support

Residence: Sixty days by plaintiff or defendant

CALIFORNIA

Grounds: Irreconcilable differences which have caused irremediable breakdown of marriage

Residence: Six months by plaintiff or defendant

COLORADO

Grounds: Adultery
Cruelty
Desertion for one year
Husband's non-support for one year
Habitual drunkenness or drug addiction for one year
Living apart for three years after decree of legal separation

Residence: One year by plaintiff or defendant, with certain exceptions

CONNECTICUT

Grounds: Adultery
Cruelty

Desertion for two years

Habitual intemperance

Residence: One year by plaintiff or defendant, with certain exceptions

DELAWARE

Grounds: Adultery

Cruelty

Desertion for one year

Husband's non-support

Habitual drunkenness for two years

Incompatibility for two years

Voluntary separation for 18 months

Residence: Two years by plaintiff or defendant, with certain exceptions

DISTRICT OF COLUMBIA

Grounds: Adultery

Desertion for one year

Voluntary separation for one year

Where the decree of legal separation has been granted for any of the above grounds or for cruelty and the separation continues for one year, the innocent spouse may apply to have the separation enlarged to absolute divorce

Residence: One year by plaintiff or defendant

FLORIDA

Grounds: Adultery

Cruelty

Desertion for one year

Habitual intemperance or use of narcotics

Residence: Six months by plaintiff

GEORGIA

Grounds: Adultery

Cruelty

Desertion for one year

Habitual intoxication

Residence: Six months by plaintiff or defendant

HAWAII

Grounds: Adultery

Cruelty

Desertion for six months

Habitual drunkenness or habitual excessive use of drugs for one year

Husband's non-support for 60 days

Expiration of term in decree of separate bed and board without reconciliation

Living separate and apart under decree of separate maintenance for more than two years without reconciliation

Voluntarily living separate and apart continuously for three years and no reasonable likelihood of resuming cohabitation, and court satisfied divorce would not be harsh, oppressive or contrary to public interest

Residence: One year by plaintiff or defendant

IDAHO

Grounds: Adulteryㅤ
Cruelty
Desertion
Willful neglect
Habitual intemperance
Living apart for five years

Residence: Six weeks by plaintiff

ILLINOIS

Grounds: Adultery
Cruelty
Desertion for one year
Habitual drunkenness or excessive use of addictive drugs for two years

Residence: One year by plaintiff, with certain exceptions

INDIANA

Grounds: Adultery
Cruelty
Desertion for two years
Habitual drunkenness
Husband's non-support for two years

Residence: One year by plaintiff or defendant

IOWA

Grounds: Adultery
Cruelty

Desertion for two years

Chronic alcoholism

Residence: One year by plaintiff, with certain exceptions

KANSAS

Grounds: Adultery

Cruelty

Desertion for one year

Gross neglect of duty

Incompatibility

Habitual drunkenness

Residence: Six months by plaintiff

KENTUCKY

Grounds: Adultery

Cruelty

Desertion for one year

Living apart for five years

Husband's habitual drunkenness for one year plus non-support

Residence: One year by plaintiff

LOUISIANA

Grounds: Adultery

Living apart for two years

Expiration of one year (14 months if guilty party applies) after decree of legal separation for adultery, cruelty, desertion, non-support,

Voluntary living apart for one year

Residence: Divorce will not be granted unless legal separation has been decreed and one year has elapsed thereafter, with certain exceptions

MAINE

Grounds: Adultery

Cruelty

Desertion for three years

Habitual intoxication or drug addiction

Husband's non-support

Residence: Six months by plaintiff, with certain exceptions

MARYLAND

Grounds: Adultery

Desertion for 18 months

Voluntary separation for 18 months

Living apart for five years

Residence: One year by plaintiff or defendant

MASSACHUSETTS

Grounds: Adultery

Cruelty

Desertion for two years

Intoxication by drugs or liquor

Husband's non-support

Residence: Two years by plaintiff, with certain exceptions

MICHIGAN

Grounds: Adultery

Cruelty

Desertion for two years

Husband's non-support

Residence: One year by plaintiff, with certain exceptions

MINNESOTA

Grounds: Adultery

Cruelty

Desertion for one year

Habitual drunkenness for one year

Continuous separation under decree of limited divorce for more than five years

Continuous separation under decree of separate maintenance for two years

Residence: One year by plaintiff, with certain exceptions

MISSISSIPPI

Grounds: Adultery

Cruelty

Desertion for one year

Habitual drunkenness or excessive use of drugs

Residence: One year by plaintiff or defendant

MISSOURI

Grounds: Adultery

Cruelty

Desertion for one year

Habitual drunkenness for one year

Residence: One year by plaintiff, with certain exceptions

MONTANA

Grounds: Adultery
Physical cruelty
Mental cruelty for one year
Desertion or neglect for one year
Habitual intemperance for one year

Residence: One year by plaintiff

NEBRASKA

Grounds: Adultery
Cruelty
Desertion for two years
Habitual drunkenness
Husband's non-support

Residence: One to two years by plaintiff, depending on circumstances, with certain exceptions

NEVADA

Grounds: Adultery
Cruelty
Desertion for one year
Habitual gross drunkenness plus incapacity to contribute to family's support
Husband's non-support
Incompatibility
Living apart for one year (in the discretion of the court)

Residence: Six weeks by plaintiff or defendant, with certain exceptions

NEW HAMPSHIRE

Grounds: Adultery
Cruelty
Habitual drunkenness for two years
Desertion for two years

Residence: One year by plaintiff, with certain exceptions

NEW JERSEY

Grounds: Adultery
Cruelty which occurred six months before suit filed
Desertion for two years

Residence: Two years by plaintiff or defendant, with certain exceptions

NEW MEXICO

Grounds: Adultery
Cruelty
Desertion
Habitual drunkenness
Husband's non-support
Incompatibility

Residence: One year

NEW YORK

Grounds: Adultery
Cruelty
Desertion for two years

Living apart for two years pursuant to a separation decree

Living apart for two years pursuant to written separation agreement

Residence: One to two years by plaintiff or defendant, depending on the circumstances, with certain exceptions

NORTH CAROLINA

Grounds: Adultery

Living apart for one year, provided no fault (proviso written in by court)

Residence: Six months by plaintiff or defendant

NORTH DAKOTA

Grounds: Adultery

Cruelty

Desertion for one year

Willful neglect or habitual intemperance for one ear

Residence: One year by plaintiff

OHIO

Grounds: Adultery

Cruelty

Desertion for one year

Gross neglect of duty

Habitual drunkenness

Residence: One year by plaintiff

OKLAHOMA

Grounds: Adultery
Cruelty
Desertion for one year
Gross neglect of duty
Incompatibility
Habitual drunkenness

Residence: Six months by plaintiff or defendant

OREGON

Grounds: Adultery
Cruelty
Desertion for one year
Habitual and gross drunkenness for one year

Residence: One year by plaintiff

PENNSYLVANIA

Grounds: Adultery
Cruelty
Desertion for two years

Residence: One year by plaintiff or defendant

PUERTO RICO

Grounds: Adultery
Cruelty
Desertion for one year
Habitual drunkenness or continued and excessive use of drugs

Living apart for three years

Residence: One year by plaintiff, with certain exceptions

RHODE ISLAND

Grounds: Adultery

Cruelty

Desertion for five years or for shorter period, in he discretion of the court

Continued drunkenness

Habitual excessive and intemperate use of drugs

Husband's non-support for one year

Living apart for 10 years in the discretion of the court

Any other gross behavior and wickedness epugnant to the marriage covenant

Residence: Two years by plaintiff or defendant

SOUTH CAROLINA

Grounds: Adultery

Cruelty

Desertion for one year

Habitual drunkenness or use of drugs

Living apart for three years

Residence: One year by plaintiff or defendant

SOUTH DAKOTA

Grounds: Adultery

Cruelty

Desertion for one year

Willful neglect for one year

Habitual intemperance for one year

Residence: One year by plaintiff, with certain exceptions

TENNESSEE

Grounds: Adultery

Desertion for one year

Habitual drunkenness

Expiration of two years after separation decree for cruelty or desertion and non-support

Residence: One year by plaintiff

TEXAS

Grounds: Adultery

Cruelty

Desertion for three years

Living apart for three years

Residence: One year by plaintiff

UTAH

Grounds: Adultery

Cruelty

Desertion for one year

Non-support

Habitual drunkenness

Separation for three years after decree of separate maintenance

Residence: Three months by plaintiff or defendant

VERMONT

Grounds: Adultery
Intolerable severity
Desertion for three years
Husband's non-support
Living apart from spouse without fault for three years

Residence: Six months by plaintiff

VIRGINIA

Grounds: Adultery
Desertion for one year
Living apart for two years
If legal separation decreed for cruelty or desertion, after one year it may be enlarged by plaintiff or defendant

Residence: One year by plaintiff or defendant

VIRGIN ISLANDS

Grounds: Adultery
Cruelty
Desertion for one year
Habitual gross drunkenness for one year
Incompatibility of temperament

Residence: Six weeks by plaintiff

WASHINGTON

Grounds: Adultery

Cruelty
Desertion for one year
Habitual drunkenness
Husband's non-support
Living apart for two years
Residence: One year

WEST VIRGINIA

Grounds: Adultery
Cruelty
Desertion for one year
Habitual drunkenness or drug addiction
Living apart for two years
Residence: One year by plaintiff or defendant

WISCONSIN

Grounds: Adultery
Cruelty
Desertion for one year
Habitual drunkenness
Husband's non-support
Voluntary separation on the part of both spouses for five years
Living apart for five years after a judgment of egal separation
Residence: Two years by plaintiff or defendant

WYOMING

Grounds: Adultery

Cruelty

Desertion for one year

Habitual drunkenness

Husband's non-support for one year

Living apart for two years provided separation was not induced or justified by cause chargeable in whole or in part to party seeking divorce

Residence: Sixty days by plaintiff, with certain exceptions

CANADA
(All provinces)

Grounds: Adultery

Cruelty

Living apart for three years (five years if person seeking divorce deserted his spouse) and thus permanent breakdown of the marriage

Residence: One year by plaintiff or defendant

MEXICO
(State of Chihuahua, City of Juarez)

Grounds: Adultery

Cruelty

Desertion for three months

Incompatibility

Non-support

Separation for one year without seeking a divorce

Written mutual consent

Residence: Requirements in process of change; consult your lawyer.

INDEX

INDEX

71 72 73 10 9 8 7 6 5 4 3 2 1